PASSION, PURITY and POPULARITY

A Daughter of Christ

By Whitney Fee

Acknowledgements

I could go on for days thanking people for their sweet words, editing, picture taking skills, and willingness to want to promote this book to save girls from the strongholds in our culture. I will try to go in order by thanking God for this incredible opportunity and for using me to help teenage girls. Next, I could not do much without the love and support of my family. To my incredible mother, Debbie Fee, you are so beautiful and always speak truth to me. Thank you for always making it a number one priority to be my mother first and my friend second. You are my best friend and the best mother any daughter could ask for. To my dad, Gene Fee, how our relationship has blossomed over the years. You have always supported 100% of the things I have done and have been there to see all my successes and failures. Thank you for always being there, taking our family on fun vacations, providing for us, and raising us in a Godly home. You are an incredible father who I love to hangout with and get advice from! Kyle, my amazing brother, thank you for just loving me and being such a great example of a teenager who loves the Lord and respects girls. To my grandparents, Phebe and Boyer Fee, you have been there for me every minute. Your love is shown in your generosity, care, and your determination to keep up with technology. I just want to say I am proud that my grandma and grandpa are on facebook and are still kids at heart. Wow! I am so grateful for the fun times you provide every time we visit and the great advice you give from your heart. You are incredible and so inspiring. Thank you for always being there and understanding what I am going through! Thank you to the other Fees who have helped edit my book, especially my cousin Katie. Your insights were amazing and I am so proud of you!

I want to thank all my college friends and sorority sisters who loved me, gave me confidence, and showed me the passion God has given me to help other girls. THANK YOU! I also want to thank NorthPoint church for allowing me to work with their high school students this past summer. Thank you Lauren, Clay, Tony, and Reese for letting me interrupt your class and use your students as role models to others. Thank you students for giving your testimonies and willingness to be in the photo shoot. Tony, thank you for inspiring me and for always believing in me. Also thank you KJ for introducing me to an amazing group of people. You all were key motivators in God's desire for me to write this book after our Memorial Day worship weekend. Thank you Lindsay Davis for drawing the logo and for your sweet heart. Thank you Tracy for taking the beautiful beach pictures! Thank you Beth Ann and Jill for your edits and for Orangewood and all your encouragement. Thank you to those incredible mentors God has put in my life: Coach Cox, Mr. Miller, Mrs. Fraas, Rob Mitchell, Beda, Angie, David

Lorenz, Meghan Maloy, Ashleigh Miller and Jenny Kellems. Also to three ministers who I admire so much: Andy Stanley, Beth Moore, and Perry Noble. Finally, thank you to my home church, Warren Baptist and Tom Sorrells in helping me launch this book! It's all because of Jesus! Thank You!

This Book is Dedicated to God.
Our father who sent His only son,
Jesus, to die for our sins.
Thank you, Lord!

Table of Contents

Chapter 1

1. Intro

Hey girls! Thanks for picking this book up and reading it. I really believe this book can change your life if you let it.

First of all, I just want to say I am sorry. I want to apologize to you for all the things the world is telling you to do and believe. Actually, what the world is telling you is to grow up and act four years older than your age. I am here to tell you to enjoy your middle school or high school years. In this book, I will tell you how you can enjoy and have great teenage years. These years won't last long, and as awkward as they can be, being an adult is just as awkward. I promise! Every adult still struggles with wanting to fit in, wanting to be accepted, and wanting to make friends.

This book will be a fun and easy read. I even got some hot high school guys to tell you what they really think about girls and share their stories. When you are finished reading, you can email me about what you liked most about the book, or share your stories with me at passionpuritypopularity@gmail.com.

I am able to share a lot about what a teenage girl looks like, because I was in your shoes a few years ago. I am 23 years old now and have taken notes on how to succeed and fail in your teenage years. I was not very popular in high school, but in college I discovered who God made me to be and was crowned Homecoming Queen of my amazing college in 2008. I have had so many doubts, insecurities, unfulfilled worldly desires and heartbreaks.

As I share with you, it is perfectly fine to disagree with me, but please ask God what He would do. Ask your mom, dad or wise adult mentor what they think. If your mom isn't present, supportive, or helpful, please let me know. I will help you find a great motherly mentor. Friends will come and go, but your family and God are here to stay.

I want to be there for you because I know this can be difficult. I know the pressures that are out there. There is pressure to be skinny. There is pressure to wear cute clothes. There is pressure to act cool. There is pressure to have the latest and greatest things or designer brands. There is pressure to like a guy. There is pressure to listen to your friends. There is pressure to do what your parents want you to do. There is pressure to tell people what they want you to tell them (even if it is a lie). There is pressure to be liked and to be accepted by others.

Oh my, this is making me stressed out telling you how many pressures are being thrown in your face every day. I feel like screaming … AHHHHHHH and saying GET ME OUT OF THIS!

Can you list five pressures you feel right now? (Please list in the space below.)

I know. It's so confusing. You are still trying to figure out what you want and who you want to be. Well, I want to assure you the things you're thinking and feeling are the same things thousands of other girls are thinking and feeling too! Do you mind if I help you out a little? All I ask is for you to read the whole book and write answers under the few questions I ask. Then, after you have read it, if you would like to stay in contact with me, please join my website (www.passionpurity-popularity.com) and please click the "give me your info" link. You can also read my blog. You can even become a fan on my Facebook page at http://www.facebook.com/pages/Passion-Purity-and-Popularity/1 26346370729514. I would love for you to send me messages and let me know what is going on in your life.

It is said that middle school is the time in teens' lives when they start to look toward their peers and friends, before they turn to their parents. The only problem is that your peers and friends don't have the wisdom to be able to give you advice on many tough subjects. I also know many of you feel you cannot talk to your parents about certain things. We will talk about that later. That is why I am here!

We will talk about being teased, not fitting in, trying to be cool, sex, boys, parents, your period and so much more. So get comfortable and let us discover the mysteries of being a girl together! By the way, I am inserting pictures of me when I was in middle school so you can see that I had braces too, frizzy hair (that is why it is always in a ponytail), and was an ordinary teenage girl. Enjoy!

P.S. Everything I am saying, I am saying only because I care about you. I want to help you avoid the traps that have already been set up for you. Thank you for letting me share my life and, hopefully, impact yours.

Chapter 2

2. Oprah Hair

When I was in the 7th grade, I had a boyfriend who was more popular than I was. He asked me out, and by the second week was already telling me he loved me. He was also a class clown in a lot of ways, and kept doing really silly things at school. I told my mom and she told me I should break up with him. She said he was too immature. So, the next day, I broke up with him. Then the drama began!

Since he was popular, many of his friends ganged up against me. One day when I was coming out of the bathroom, he told me my hair looked like Oprah's hair. I was so shocked that I did not know what to say, but obviously his friends overheard and they all started laughing at me. There was nowhere for me to escape because our class was headed to the library. So, I ignored them while my tears built up. I could not believe the guy who told me he loved me two days ago was now making fun of me. Don't get me wrong, Oprah is great, but at the age of 12, I did not want Oprah hair.

That afternoon when I got home, I ran upstairs to tell my mom. Before one word could even come out, a waterfall was flowing from my eyes. A girl can give you a mean comment and you just think she is jealous, but when a guy gives you a mean comment, it tears you up inside. I believe when a guy compliments a girl, it means 10 times more to her, but when he teases, it makes her feel 10 times worse than if a girl had said it.

My mom said he was immature, like she told me before, and that what my ex-boyfriend had said was not true. My mother's words did not make me feel much better, but it was still nice to tell someone who cared about me. Then my mom hugged me, but it only helped a little. A mother can put a Band-Aid on your bleeding wound to make it stop bleeding, but the wound is still there. Sometimes you just have to learn how to take things and deal with them, but do not let it get you down, because you are "fearfully and wonderfully made" by God (Psalm 139:14).

Maybe he was just trying to get my attention like Liam Hemsworth, an actor in *The Last Song*, tells *Seventeen* about his first crush. He says, "In first grade, I had a friend called Amanda. I probably treated her more mean than nice, because I didn't know what to do. We'd throw sticks at her across the playground—anything to get her attention!" (*Seventeen* 123)

Really? I cannot believe guys think a girl will assume he likes her because he threw sticks at her. Apparently this is how guys show they care in their early years. So maybe this was the case with my ex-boy-friend, because he did not stop at calling me Oprah.

The next day, I was in class with my ex-boyfriend and he grabbed my purse and started looking through it. First of all, I recommend never letting a guy go through your purse. Well, of course, he found a "girl object" in my purse and began to pull it out. As soon as he lifted his hand out of my purse, the teacher called him up to her desk. She wrote him up for detention and told him to grow up! Ha. Well, that was all the disciplining he needed, because after that he never really talked to me again, and I was glad. But the teasing did not end there.

I also had a teacher one day ask me to stand up in front of the class and do whatever he told me to do. (Now, just so you know, I was a very quiet girl and I never really spoke up in class. This particular teacher scared me to death! I dreaded the class and never felt comfortable there. Also, the teacher was a retired military officer, if that helps to explain the intimidation I felt.) So, I stood up in front of the class as he yelled orders at me. For some reason, I did not understand what he wanted me to do. Probably because I was so scared and about to pee in my pants. So he continued yelling commands at me and then told me to just sit down and that I was no help to him. I just wanted to dig a really big hole, crawl inside, and never, ever come out.

I was so upset for many reasons. First, I tried really hard to do well in that class and I felt like the teacher never realized it. I felt like he thought I was stupid. Second, the one time he asked me to do some-thing, I failed. Third, he embarrassed me by yelling at me in front of the class. So, in a matter of two minutes, I was stupid, a failure, and the most embarrassed I had ever been. Needless to say, when I got home I ran to my room, headed straight to my closet, and shut the doors. This time I wasn't crying a waterfall, but rather the entire Atlantic Ocean. I know you think I am a crybaby, but those are really the only two times I ever remember crying at that age.

My mom heard me and walked into my room. I never went into my closet to hide, so she asked what happened. I told her and in a matter of a minute, she was on the phone with the principal. She set up an appointment for her and my dad to speak with him. I was a sweet girl in school, a good student, and my mom was sticking up for me when I did not have the strength. The next morning, my mom and dad had a meeting with the principal and teacher. The teacher said he felt awful and was very sorry. After the meeting, while I was in chorus class, the mean teacher asked if I could come with him. That was even more embarrassing, because no one goes on a walk with him. I am sure this started gossip that I didn't even know about.

When we got back to his classroom, he said, "Whitney, I am very sorry. I just spoke with your parents and you are the last person in the world that I would ever want to hurt. You are a great student and a sweet girl. Please forgive me." He then continued to tell me how this had impacted his life and helped him see how his children might view him. Because my parents stood up to him and explained how I felt, it then taught him a great lesson in how to better treat other teenagers, including his children. Wow!

Of course I said I forgave him, with tears in my eyes, and he wrote me a pass to do whatever I needed to before I returned to class. So, I learned not only do peers tease you, but many times adults and family can, too. Usually adults do not aim to hurt you, especially your parents and teachers. I also learned that once people find out how awful their words made you feel, many times they stop and apologize. If they continue to bully you, then remember this saying: "Mean girls and boys make mean men and women." They will never get far in life, because no one will trust them or want to be around them. People want to be around sweet people, caring people, thoughtful people, and loving people.

The main reason teasing hurts us so much is because we have this intense desire to be accepted. When you are teased, it is the opposite of being accepted. It causes you to doubt yourself, and you feel defeated. Teasing can rip our hearts, if we let it. The problem is that many times when it happens, we have no control. I had no control over being teased about my hair or being made fun of in front of the class. People were letting words come out of their mouths that should not have. Proverbs 4: 23-25 says, "Guard your heart above all else, for it determines the course of your life. Avoid all perverse (bad) talk; stay away from corrupt speech. Look straight ahead, and fix your eyes on what lies before you."

When I conducted an informal questionnaire with a group of senior high school guys, I asked them if they had ever been teased before. Out of the group, 72.7% said they had been teased to the extent that it made them very hurt and angry. To add to that, these are very popular guys who are well-respected and admired. Even the popular, hot, cool-looking guys are made fun of and ridiculed to the extent that they are embarrassed and offended.

So what do you do when you are teased? What would you have done if you were in my shoes? (Write about it here.)

My advice is to talk to a trusted adult (parents, teacher, counselor, or adult mentor) about the teasing incident that recently occurred. He or she can give you strong advice and will keep your feelings to themselves, unlike your friends, who will probably tell other people. If I would not have had a mother or another older female role model to turn to, then who knows what would have happened? Older women have experienced similar things and they will help you through the battle. I know that it takes 10 compliments to equal one negative comment, but a loving older woman will give you 100 compliments if that is what it takes to build you back up again. If you turn to your friends, they will probably say, "He's stupid. Just get over it." Or, they might tell other people, and then all of a sudden your problem becomes a disaster because the entire school knows, or at least it feels that way. I hope that the mentor of your choosing tells you what God says about the situation.

P.S. God is COOL and loving Jesus will only make your life 100x better.

While Jesus was on the earth, He was teased by many, especially the Roman soldiers. They spat on Him, made fun of Him, and mocked the things He said. What would Jesus do? Jesus first felt sorry for them, because He knew that they did not know how much it hurt Him. Then, Jesus would always retreat and go pray to God. When you are going through tough times, do you pray to God? God thinks you are awesome and He wants to help you. Do you ask God to help you? If you do, God will respond. "Take delight in the Lord, and He will give you your heart's desires," Psalm 37:4. Many times, I feel so helpless and alone, so I pray to God to help me feel safe and secure. I also ask for strength and God ALWAYS rescues me. Here is another great verse to remember: "And the Spirit helps us in our weakness. For example, we don't know what God wants us to pray for. But the Holy Spirit prays for us with groanings that cannot be expressed in words," Romans 8:26.

God loves you and has great plans for you (Jeremiah 29:11). It will help you to truly believe this and to know that those great plans for you will happen soon. Get excited!

Do you think God has a great life planned for you? (Write about it here.)

Do you think this plan can only happen if you make the right choices? (Write about it here.)

Do you ever pray to God and ask Him to rescue you from the evil things around you?

(Please respond here with a Yes or No and why you gave your answer.)

God gives us free will to make our own decisions. That is why He gave us the Holy Spirit, because without the Holy Spirit living in us, we would have no clue what to do. However, we miss out when we forget to pray and ask God to help us through the day. Every day, we should ask God to fill the empty places in our hearts with His love. Be honest and open with God, confess your sins or mistakes, and ask God to protect you throughout your day. He will give you an unspeakable joy and peace that can only be obtained through asking Him.

"Commit everything you do to the Lord. Trust him, and He will help you. He will make your innocence radiate like the dawn, and the justice of your cause will shine like the noonday sun. Be still in the presence of the Lord, and wait patiently for Him to act. Don't worry about evil people who prosper, or fret about their wicked schemes. Stop being angry! Turn from your rage! Do not lose your temper—it only leads to harm. For the wicked will be destroyed; but those who trust in the Lord will possess the land. Soon the wicked will disappear. Though you look for them, they will be gone. The lowly will possess the land and will live in peace and prosperity." Psalm 37: 5-11.

Chapter 3

3. Friends

Finding friends and keeping friends can be awkward or scary at times. Many times you make a good friend by having a class together, but then what happens next year if she is in a different class? You don't see her as much, so now you will have to figure out how to hang out outside of school. What if you see a girl in class who looks really sweet, but you don't know if she will like you? What should you do? Well, in this case, I would ask her if she would like to come over to my house sometime, or to do something together. Many people won't tell you this, but it means a lot to a person if you ask them to hang out. It shows that you care and think they are a cool person. It takes boldness, but the worst they can do is say "no." Most people might not want to hang out every afternoon, so it is good to hang out once or twice a week. Then you have time for other things you like to do and spend time with other friends. It is hard for the average person to have more than 3 – 4 best friends at one given time, so don't stress yourself out. Evaluate your friends and think about who is better to be around. Then invite them to hangout with you during the week.

In middle school I was known as the shy girl, but in one of my classes I sat next to a popular girl. She was very sweet to me and we would talk about hanging out, although we never did. I assumed it was because she thought she was too cool to hang out with me after school, but I think it was as much my fault as hers. I never officially invited her to do a specific thing together. We would just say, "We should hangout sometime" and that was it. I blame my shyness for holding me back. So, if you are shy, I want to give you some tips that will help you through your teen years. First of all, you have to ask yourself "What scares me?" For me, the popular people intimidated me. I thought they were always judging me, but I assumed that was what they were thinking when they probably weren't. Many times, we have to recognize that the world is not looking at us, because most people are too busy thinking about themselves. This is sad, but true. Next, you should focus on things you do well, such as talents and strengths. If you are a good dancer, then work to be even better and be proud of that. If you are a great runner, then keep up the great work and be confident in the talents God gave you. Third, it is ok to stand out, to be different, and to be a sweet girl instead of a mean girl. If you are always trying to fit in, it will leave you stressed and aggravated. Remember, to be happy with who you are; remember that people are just thinking about themselves; and continue to make new friends who are fun and good girls.

Another reason people will always love to hang around you is if you compliment them. People love to feel loved. So, if you tell Suzy that she looks pretty today, it will mean so much to her even if it doesn't seem like it. I used to have a hard time accepting compliments, but now I have learned to say thank you and then compliment them back in the future. It is a "Pay it Forward" exercise. When someone does or says something nice to you, you should then say something nice to another person in return. Wouldn't the world be a nicer place if everyone loved others as much as they love themselves.

Another way to gain confidence and lose stress is by working out. This releases stored energy and hormones into the body, which leads to a balanced life and better focus. It's been said that if exercise were a drug, it would be the most powerful medication on earth. Here are 10 other benefits from howtobefit.com: Exercise can reduce the impact of stress, release negative energy and is a good way to manage anger. It offers calmness, the ability to recharge so you can better deal with conflict and problem solving, reduces muscle discomfort, helps you not get depressed, increases awareness, decreases boredom, improves your sleep time, and you will have a stronger immune system. ("HowToBeFit.Com")

Now, with exercise and believing in who you are, the next step would be to see and visualize yourself as a confident and happy person. Beth Moore once said, "Victorious lives flow through victorious thoughts." Confidence is shown through the proper posture of sitting up straight, walking with a purpose, and knowing that God is going to give you the very best. It is even better when people affirm or compliment you, because words can be so powerful and encouraging. Another way to increase boldness is to stay in a safe, uncomfortable situation to learn how to react when things are awkward. This can be good practice for you to turn a boring situation into a fun environment. For instance, say you are in a church or school group and everyone is bored. Instead of leaving, you could ask people to tell about their favorite vacation, their favorite TV show, or hobbies they enjoy. However, if you are in an uncomfortable situation that involves drugs, alcohol, or sex, please run out of there as soon as possible. I would sneak out so you are not causing a scene or act like you have to step outside to take a phone call and then run! Also, remember that not everyone will like you. It is better to learn this lesson early. Many times it isn't you they don't like, it is probably your personalities that clash or you just don't agree on anything. God made everyone different for a reason, so accept your differences and meet other people. Lastly, label yourself with positive words and practice socializing with others. It is better to socialize in person, although online social media is huge right now. I encourage you to go to church more often, go on retreats, go to summer camps, volunteer in your community, and allow your list of friends to double in size as you meet new people.

The number one lesson I have learned on shyness and insecurity is the importance of feeling free of strongholds (things that keep us from being who we want to be). Free from friends who put you down, free from classes when the summer comes, and free from strongholds that keep you in an emotional prison. A stronghold is anything of this world that you put before God. It is a stronghold, because it is hard to let go of it and allow God to be in control. For many girls, a boyfriend is a stronghold. For others, an excess of money, a cigarette or an eating disorder is a stronghold. Dating can easily become a god in your life. Satan loves for us to have these strongholds because he uses them to strangle the life out of us. The problem is that many of these strongholds have been forming over many years to where it's hard to figure out what is keeping you from feeling the freedom in Christ. A simple way to figure out your stronghold is by asking: What in life can I not live without?

Please list below your strongholds (things you put before God):

Satan is very tricky. The Bible says, "Be self-controlled and alert. Your enemy the devil prowls around like a roaring lion looking for someone to devour" 1 Peter 5:8. We must always be on guard, because he is prowling and waiting for someone to destroy. Satan is the meanest villain you could ever imagine. He wants awful things to happen to you and laughs at you when they do. God has compassion for you and is always waiting to give you the biggest and best hug ever. The way Satan tricks us is by allowing us to rationalize or come up with excuses as to why we have strongholds or things that we must have in order to live. I know we must have food, water, and clothing, but God promises He will provide those things when you are in His will. He says, "So don't worry about these things, saying, 'What will you eat? What will we drink? What will we wear? These things dominate the thoughts of unbelievers, but your heavenly Father already knows all your needs. Seek the Kingdom of God above all else, and live righteously, and he will give you everything you need. So don't worry about tomorrow, for tomorrow will bring its own worries. Today's trouble is enough for today," Matthew 6:31-34.

Psalm 46:1 says, "God is our refuge and strength, always ready to help in times of trouble."

The moral of the story is that we should not worry. Worry only causes problems and can create lots of drama. I once overheard a girl telling a guy, "If you want to be drama free you have to…" and then her voice died. I wanted to finish her sentence by saying, "If you want to be drama free you need to be a Christian and put others before yourself." The girl was flirting with a guy and talking about all the drama between guys and her friends. She was obviously stressed and confused. This is where it is better to avoid situations, because drama equals gossip and fights. You can always take yourself out of a situation by stating that you are not taking sides. Then you can keep both friends.

I want to end this chapter with this great statement that I hope you will post on your wall or mirror. It is from Beth Moore's book: <u>So Long, Insecurity</u>, "You can hurt my feelings, criticize me, embarrass me, intimidate or threaten me, but you cannot have my security. I won't let you. It's mine to keep. You cannot have it." My security is in Christ and he gives me such joy and freedom! If you truly believe this and act it out, so many people will admire you and want to know why you always are happy and have lots of joy. What a great person to be!

Chapter 4

4. Princess Fiona

Expectations are not facts or certainties. They are confident beliefs or strong hopes that a particular event will happen. Therefore, expectations are not always accurate. I'll explain. Let me say, for instance, that I am going to pick you up, and all I tell you is that we are going somewhere fun. What are you expecting? You could guess where I might take you, but you really have no idea.

What if I took you to a garbage dump? I bet you wouldn't expect that. Or what if I took you to Hawaii to swim with the dolphins and lay out on the beach? That would probably be better than what you would expect. Or maybe I was just planning on taking you to pick up lunch? How would you know?

Expectations are things we think or are sure will happen. Many times, we think things will happen and they do not. Sometimes, we expect things to look a certain way or we expect to have a lot of fun, and we don't.

Do you think that we put all the expectations on ourselves and never realize it? It is great to ask God to help you and give you things you need, but instead of expecting all those things to happen, we should be very happy that God gave us what He did. For instance, have you ever been shopping and told your mom or a friend that you liked something and then, on your birthday, they gave you what you pointed out in the store? You did not expect them to give it to you, but you told them you liked it and they gave it to you. This is how God works. If you ask for something, and God thinks it would be good for you, He will give it to you! He has a way with surprises. If we allow God to surprise us instead of expecting gifts from Him, then the rewards are much greater. It is a pleasant surprise when you have no expectations and someone does something for you, or you have a wonderful day when you did not expect to have one. What about when you get flowers from someone, or a sweet note? How do you feel? I think everyone would agree that when something nice happens that you don't expect or demand, it makes you feel loved and accepted. Is that not the coolest feeling? They are saying, "I really care for you and wanted to give you something nice."

I cannot tell you how many times God has rescued me from a bad situation or surprised me with something greater than I could ever imagine. God knows what you really want and need. It is also good to tell Him and pray for your desires. If you are patient and pursuing a relationship with Him, He will do even better than you could imagine.

What happens if we already have expectations? Well, then that makes it hard on God, because if He gives us something different from what we expect or think we deserve, we might get angry. For example, when I am in a relationship with a guy after a few months,

I always pray that if I am not supposed to marry Him that God will somehow break us up. Many times, God breaks up my relationships in a matter of a day after uttering this prayer. At first I am sad about the breakup, because I expected God to say "He is your perfect match." Instead, I was left single again.

I have learned over the years that God usually brings along a great guy when you are not looking for him. You can never be in a great and healthy relationship if you are not happy and content being single. God gives people mates for many reasons. When a woman gets married, her husband should be her best friend. He should help her with things around the house, help make money to live off of, and later they can have children together. Men were made to be the providers and women tend to nurture. Marriage is a great thing if each person works hard to serve and please the other person. Being married also allows the couple to have children under God's blessing. I believe you need to be happy before you date someone. You are the person who is in control of your happiness. When you are happy with who you are and you begin to date someone, then your relationship can be amazing. When you expect a guy to make you happy, he will feel the pressure you are putting on him and will probably leave you. I am not saying that you won't have bad days when you are in a relationship, but if you are always unhappy, then the guy will get frustrated and likely break up with you.

I am giving you this advice because I have fallen into the trap of expecting God to make my hopes and dreams come true. However,

God sometimes has bigger hopes and dreams than we can imagine. As girls, we say, "I expect you to give me this thing. I expect you to make this guy like me. I expect you to help me make all A's on my test that I did not study well for." I am so guilty, too. It is hard to think that God would not want you to have something that you think is good. Instead, you should tell God what you desire and then let Him give you what you really need in the form of a present. As my cousin would say, "moral of the story is don't demand anything from God, but you should ask him." Once again, I catch myself doing this all the time, and the days when I let God surprise me are always more fun, exciting, and rewarding.

Here is another personal example. My brother always reminds me of it. You will see why in a second. Every year when it is our birthday, the birthday guy or girl gets to choose where they want to go eat. Well, on my 14th birthday, I was getting ready and my brother came to my door and said, "Hurry up, we are ready and we are going to eat at TGI Friday's."

I replied, "No we are not. It is my birthday and I get to pick wherever I want to go."

He laughed and said, "No, we already decided, and we are going to TGI Friday's."

Well, I had never hit my little brother before, but this time I did. I hit him on the head and said, "FINE!" (P.S. Please do not think it is ok to hit your brother. Although, we laugh about it now.) So, we get in the car and I am very upset. I could not believe my parents would not let me decide where to go eat on my birthday. They knew I loved to pick the restaurant. You see, I had the expectation of being able to choose where I wanted to eat, and this was the only way my special day would be perfect.

When we got to TGI Friday's, I jumped out of the car and told the hostess, "Four."

My parents were walking fast, trying to catch up, and I did not understand why they were in such a hurry. By the time the waitress grabbed four menus, my mom said, "Sorry, we are actually with the party."

I turned and said, "What are you talking about?"

She turned to me and said, "Look!"

This was my *Oh My Goodness* moment. About 20 of my best friends were sitting at a table waiting for me. Immediately, they yelled, "SURPRISE!"

I was surprised for sure, and it was one of the best birthdays ever. On top of that, my mom didn't even plan it. My friends did, not knowing that TGI Friday's was not one of my favorite restaurants. That night will always bring back great memories.

Please let God surprise you. Please try not to compare yourself to others and expect God to give you what they have. You are an amazing and different person! Believe it or not, God made enough AMAZING and different surprises that each one of us can be blessed daily. We just have to trust in Him, ask, wait patiently (don't demand), and allow everything to work out in His perfect time. When the surprise comes, you will be glad you waited!

Here is another example, from the movie *Shrek*, where Princess Fiona has expectations of a prince and Shrek does not quite meet her expectations:

Princess Fiona says, "What are you doing? You know, you should sweep me off my feet out yonder window and down a rope onto your valiant steed."

After a few more exchanges in words, *Princess Fiona* replies with her expectations in mind, "But this isn't right. You're meant to charge in, sword drawn, banner flying — that's what all the other knights did."

Later, *Princess Fiona* innocently questions Shrek, "But... how will you kiss me?"

Shrek says, "What? That wasn't in the job description." (Elliot, Ted)

I love it. This is great because it describes middle school relationships perfectly. You see, girls grow up and mature faster than guys. Don't ask me why, because I am still trying to figure that one out, too. But, girls have these expectations of getting in great, romantic relationships by 8th grade and meeting the prince of their dreams. In today's time, this is not typical at all! Actually maybe less than 1% of married couples will meet that way, but most of the time you won't meet your one-and-only husband until later. People are getting married later, and middle school boys are clueless about love. I promise.

Girls, do not worry, because you should enjoy your 20s and not make it a mission to get married. Believe me. I thought I would have found the one by now, too, but actually I am glad God is teaching me patience and trust. I have been able to go on many amazing trips and do a lot more things than if I was married now. Finding a guy is an expectation girls put on themselves all the time. Even worse, when girls do not meet a guy at the right time, many get depressed, anxious, worried, and start thinking they are not beautiful or valued. This is the worst thing you could ever do to yourself. It causes eating disorders, suicide, low self-esteem, and you will be far less attractive to healthy guys. Why? After questioning several healthy guys at a gathering, many told me they look for qualities including confidence and being com-fortable in your own skin. Instead of hunting down our perfect mate, we need to let God set the expectations by the things He gives us.

Are you willing to let God surprise you?

What expectations or demands do you need to throw in the trash? God will always give you the best He has in store for you! (Write about it here)

In the meantime, enjoy having healthy friendships with guys your age. You can meet guys at school and church. Then, just enjoy hanging out. A friendship at this age is WAY BETTER than any dating rela-tionship. Also, develop a group of girls who will be great friends, but don't force friendships if the other person is too busy or doesn't want to hang out. If your friends are already getting into bad things, then now is the time to pick new friends. If you stay their friend now, it is hard to get out of those friendships later, and they will have no problem pulling you down with them. DON'T FALL INTO THEIR TRAP! But if you can confront them and recommend a trusting adult to help them, then that is PERFECT. Also, if you stand up to bad things your friends are doing, they might respect you more and want to escape the trap themselves. The more confident and stronger you are as a teenager the more mature and respected you will be as an adult. If you need help with this, don't worry because that's normal. You can talk to your mom, dad, a Christian mentor, or you can email me at *passionpuritypopularity@gmail.com*.

I loved the quote from Kiara, age 20, from Macon, GA, in *Seventeen*, "In the story, 'I'm addicted to Bad Boys,' I agreed when Erica said that guy drama (though exciting) was addictive and dangerous. But I think the biggest lesson was how she realized that she didn't need to rely on any guy to feel better about herself. She reminded me that you can be independent whether you're in a relationship or not. I don't need a guy to complete me, and knowing this makes dating so much less stressful."

It makes it less stressful because she is able to have fun with a guy without having to meet any expectations. It is ok if you don't click with a guy because you should be secure in who you are and confident that God will, one day, bring the right one to you.

Expectations will not satisfy, but surprises will blow you off your feet! Allow God to give you a rich and satisfying life like Jesus promises.

Jesus says, "The thief's (Satan's) purpose is to steal and kill and destroy. My purpose is to give them a rich and satisfying life," John 10:10.

Chapter 5

5. What Love Language do I speak?

There are several self-evaluation tests out there that can help you evaluate how to relate to others and what things can make you feel more loved. Many factors about a person's past play big roles in a person's capacity to fall in love, such as chemicals in the brain, cultural backgrounds, social factors, and how they have learned in the past. People learn from what they see. For example, some people witness their fathers giving their mothers flowers and learn that this is something that makes their mothers happy. We also learn about love from TV and movies. Many comedy shows focus around the plot of a man not pleasing his wife and once he figures out what she wants, the show ends with a make-up scene. Husbands and boyfriends learn what rewards their girlfriend or wife likes, whether it is sweet hugs, chocolate, or quality time. A guy can see the glow in a girl's eye that makes his heart melt. A great point Dr. Helen Fisher, one of this country's most prominent anthropologists, brings up is that, "If humans become conditioned by their experiences, this may be the reason why some people date the same type of partner over and over again." She says humans develop a "love map," which contains qualities he or she desires in a mate. Helen Fisher recommends not predicting the outcome of relationships, because it will make the thought of dating and marriage seem like a job application.

People can be put into four categories: Explorer, Builder, Director, and Negotiator, based on the different chemicals that are dominant in the brain. My favorite is the Five Love Languages quiz. According to Gary Chapman, The Five Love Languages are: Words of Affirmation (complimenting or encouraging another person), Quality Time, Receiving Gifts, Acts of Service (volunteering or helping around the house), and Physical Touch (hugs).

My number one love language is receiving gifts. It is not always the gift that means the most, as it is the right timing and thought that was put into the gift. This lets me know that he thought of me throughout the day and spent time to give it to me. I believe the main reason this is my top love language is because of my relationship with my father. He is a great provider and has always allowed me to pursue any dream. He has provided security for me through his financial support and has allowed my mom and me to go on special trips together and shopping. I love my dad very much, but my mom has been the one to always give me words of affirmation and advice. She pretty much claimed me in those areas, so when my dad and I talk about deep things that means a lot too, because we don't have those conversations often. You can take a love language quiz for singles or children at: *http://www.5lovelanguages. com/assessments/love/*.

By taking this quiz, it will also help you realize the type of love you desire when you need to be comforted. Do you need a hug when you are upset? Would you rather be complimented? Do you need quality time with someone? Would flowers brighten up your day? Take the test and write below what your love language is.

Only a small area of the human brain is active in love. Anger and fear occurs in different areas of the brain. In other words, "the brains of people deeply in love do not look like those of people experiencing strong emotions, but instead like those of people with addictions. This is why scientists can conclude that love is an addiction, especially with infatuation. Love comes in three flavors: lust, romantic love, and long-term attachment. Lust is characterized by physical cravings in a relationship. Romantic love is the state of being in love (obsessive thoughts about the guy). This is where depression issues can occur if there is a breakup, because rejection of love can easily cause serious depression. Helen Fisher states, "Romantic love is one of the strongest drives on Earth." It is unstable love. Lastly, long-term attachment is stable and "is characterized by feelings of calmness, security, social comfort and emotional union."

So how does divorce happen? Fisher gives one possibility: "You can feel deep attachment for a long-term spouse, while you feel romantic love for someone else. This means it is possible to love more than one person at a time, a situation that leads to jealousy, adultery and divorce."

Love is a choice, and married couples should choose to only have these feelings of love for their husband or wife. "Men are attracted to youth and beauty, while women are more attracted to money, education and position," Fisher said. These are things you will care about more, as you grow older.

6. Metamorphosis: My Body is Changing!!!

As you go through puberty, not only is your body changing, but your mind is too! If you are trying to figure out your identity, that's normal. It is also common if you get moody, because these changes can be frustrating and confusing. However, you still need to respect your parents like the Bible says. I would strongly encourage you not to talk back to your parents, yell at them, or say rude things, because in the end, they care about you the most on this earth. I realize that it is normal for your close friendships to become more important and that parents will have less of an effect on you in your teenage years. But be cautious, because wisdom is the key to happiness. If you do not want to go to your parents for wisdom, then I encourage you to read the book of Proverbs in the Bible. It is AMAZING. It teaches you great wisdom. Also, find someone who is a "hero" in your eyes, or an adult figure to look up to. I would personally choose someone I can hang out with and talk to versus a celebrity figure. I had both. I really admire Beth Moore, but I also had a great mentor in college and amazing church leaders in high school.

Also, your actions will speak louder than your words. While going through puberty, many teens show what they are thinking by how they act, rather than saying something. You begin to have these inner conversations in your head, and if you believe in Jesus, the Holy Spirit is inside you too, which is so COOL! These inner conversations are helping you to problem-solve and distinguish right from wrong.

Here is a characteristic among teens. Most young adults think they are invincible. If you believe you are conquerable, then you are probably very logical and mature for your age. Why do you think so many teenagers drink and drive? They do this because they think nothing bad will happen to them. I think this is very common for guys. They are tough to scare! When you are young, you do not realize the dangers of this world, so doing crazy, fun things seems to be smart. I see more casts and stitches on young people than I do on adults. Just think about it, and be careful. Also, it is very common for teens to think the world revolves around them, but soon reality will strike. Teens will notice that others plan to do great things too, and have dreams and goals as well. You are not the only one with a big plan for your life. Sometimes others will succeed and sometimes you will, but not everyone can win first place or the grand prize. Life can be a long competition, but if you look at it as a fun and relaxing board game, where you enjoy the time spent with friends and family, and your life will be happy, content and fulfilled. However, if you are only thinking about winning many will find you greedy and selfish. This is not a good way to make friends and live a sweet life.

Lastly, during puberty, you will learn that YOU are responsible for your relationships, not your parents, friends, teachers, or mentors. YOU are the only person who can change your mind and make the right choices. It is good to figure out early what good and bad choices are. Once you get in a bad situation, it will be easier to get out of because you have set boundaries and goals for yourself. For example, I knew that if I ever ended up in a house full of alcohol in middle or high school, then I would leave immediately, because the chances of the police breaking up the party are very, very high. Also, I knew that I wanted to wait to have sex until marriage, so I knew if at any time a guy would try to convince me to have sex, I would kick him where it hurts. I'm just kidding. No actually, I always told my boyfriends up front that if they asked me to have sex, to go ahead and assume that we are already broken up, because I will be walking out the front door immediately. You might think you will never get into these situations, but remember you are not invincible, indestructible, unbeatable, or unbreakable. Bad things happen to good people. Decide now!

What will you do when:

1. Someone asks you to go to a party where there will be alcohol? (Write about it here)

2. Someone asks you if you want a cigarette or to try a type of drug? (Write about it here)

3. A guy asks you to have sex or sleep with him? (Write about it here)

4. Name some things that you never want to happen to you: (Write about it here)

Now, pray that God will give you opportunities to be bold, to be strong, and to stand up to the evils of this world. Girls, I encourage you to go to True Love Waits online at *http://www.lifeway.com/tlw* and sign an agreement, and also buy the ring. Actually, ask your father to buy you the ring. It will mean so much to him, and he might even cry. Well, maybe cry, because he is so happy! The Bible states that unlawfulness, alcohol, drugs, and sex before marriage are all sins and traps of this world to avoid. I am praying for you now, too, and please know that you can contact me anytime. I would really love to connect with you and encourage you.

You will never have to suffer alone, and you will be way cooler if you say "No" to the bad things now rather than later. God says, "Even if we feel guilty, (I am) God is greater than our feelings, and he knows everything," 1 John 3:20. Satan and the world lies to us making us think we are in control. Many people think as long as they are good people that God will let them into heaven, but that is not how it works. No one can earn points with God. You can't earn anything, because Jesus already maxed out our points. So do not let the world make you feel guilty, but instead stick up for what you know is right!

Here are some great verses to memorize and keep near:

"Keep on asking, and you will receive what you ask for. Keep on seeking, and you will find. Keep on knocking, and the door will be opened to you. For everyone who

asks, receives. Everyone who seeks, finds. And to everyone who knocks, the door will be opened." Matthew 7:7-8.

"May you experience the love of Christ, though it is too great to understand fully. Then you will be made complete with all the fullness of life (full of Jesus' love, joy, peace, patience, kindness, goodness, faithfulness, gentleness, self-control, power, strength, faith, holiness, purity, righteousness) and power that comes from God." Ephesians 3:19.

"Anyone who believes in me may come and drink! For the Scriptures declare, 'Rivers of living water (abundant life) will flow from his (our) heart." John 7:38.

"However, those the Father has given me will come to me, and I will never reject them." John 6:37.

"The Lord will guide you continually, giving you water when you are dry and restoring your strength. You will be like a well-watered garden, like an ever-flowing spring," Isaiah 58:11.

What great promises God has given us! The best part about it is that God always fulfills His promises and never takes them back. You can ALWAYS count on God.

Chapter 7

7. Crazy Love: Five Tips About Love, Guys, Dating and Relationships

Sometimes I feel like Giselle in the movie *Enchanted*. She falls into New York City from a fairytale world of Andalasia and she is clueless. She is clueless about how relationships work in New York and asks things like, "Why are they getting a divorce, don't they love each other?" I personally love Giselle, because she is sweet and innocent, but tells the world of her wisdom on love. Remember the song, "That's How you Know"? The song takes place in Central Park, where she is singing about how you will know that he loves you. Well, she is right. She speaks about acts of kindness that a man would do if he really cared for you, and that is what every girl should expect! This would be a good expectation, because God would never want you to be with someone who would hurt you physically or with harsh words. Girls should not go after guys. Guys should chase girls. When you are patient and allow a guy to chase you, God will, one day, bring a guy who is so honored to pursue you. (Kelly, Bill)

I must admit, teenage magazines have seemed to clean up their act quite nicely. I was expecting to open up *Seventeen* Magazine and want to close it immediately, but instead I was saying "Way to Go, That's Right!" The only inappropriate article I found was, "Have Your Hottest Summer Hook Up" (Benson 96). It was such a gushy article of quotes from girls about infatuation. That's what makes dating hard. Infatuation is when you are so crazy about a person you ignore all the red flags. It is being obsessed with a boy, because he is so hot, so popular, and says the right things, etc. However, if you dig deeper and the guy does not have the same level of maturity, spiritual strength, a desire to lead, or genuine care for you, then you need to be very careful. He most likely will not stay around for long, especially if he does not trust you or respect the decisions you have made.

In the *Seventeen* article, "Have Your Hottest Summer hookup" one girl talks about finding a guy while on vacation. She says that she believes it is the perfect place to meet someone, because you are already relaxed. I, however, think this is when you can get in trouble, because you are not on your guard. Satan will attack you when you are not alert and when you are too relaxed. Surprisingly, most people think about relationships with the opposite sex more than anything else during an average day. Girls daydream about finding that great guy or when they will get to hang out with their boyfriend next. These thoughts invade our mind and can really confuse. Girls, never forget that, above all else, you must GUARD YOUR HEART!

Jordan an 18-year-old guy from Cleburn, TX, said, "Let him chase you. I met this beautiful girl on a cruise, but she never acted interested. Then on our last night, at sunset, she whispered that she'd thought about me the whole trip. I couldn't believe it. The soft kiss that came next was perfect." I bet the reason the girl waited to tell him on the last day was because if he did not like her back, then it was ok, because they would be getting off the boat in the morning. I am glad he described their kiss as soft. There is no reason to get physically or emotionally attached to someone when you will never see him or her again. I would have suggested a sweet hug instead, but I am glad it was still innocent.

In *Seventeen*'s June/July 2010 (Vol. 69, No.7) issue, Justin Bieber was asked, "What kind of girls are you drawn to?" He answers: "Someone who's funny. I like to laugh. But I need someone smart. I don't want to talk to someone who's dumb. I want to have an actual conversation with a girl, and I don't want it to feel like I'm interviewing her. I don't want to have to ask her what her favorite color is."

He was also asked, "Have you ever been in love?" He responded, "I've loved girls before, but I haven't been in love. There's a big difference. I don't know what love feels like yet. It's like, if you'd never had chocolate before, you couldn't guess the taste of it. But I would love to fall in love." He is right where he should be for his age. Love is complicated and crazy. You should never seriously date until college, when you have been fully able to mature and know who God has made you to be.

God already showed us what happens when a female takes the lead in a relationship. He told us at the very beginning of the Bible in Genesis, when Eve told Adam what to do. Eve suggested eating from the Tree of the Knowledge of Good and Evil because Satan convinced her that it would be better for her. Satan does this to us everyday, and we do not even realize it. We pursue our own desires, including trying to get a guy's attention, and many times we fall right into Satan's trap.

Genesis 3:6-7 says, "The woman was convinced. She saw that the tree was beautiful and its fruit looked delicious, and she wanted the wisdom it would give her. So she took some of the fruit and ate it. Then she gave some to her husband, who was with her, and he ate it too. At that moment their eyes were opened, and they suddenly felt shame at their nakedness. So they sewed fig leaves together to cover themselves." Satan tempted Eve and then Eve tempted Adam. Adam knew better, but instead of rejecting the fruit, Adam tasted the fruit as well. I bet Eve had a bad feeling about eating the fruit, but because she felt pressured by Satan, she did it anyway. This all caused sin to fall into every person's marriage and relationships. There is no perfect love, because of sin. However, your love will be better protected if you allow a guy to pursue you, if you respect him, and then allow him to protect and learn to love you.

Here are 5 great dating tips:

Tip #1: Wait on God. As I suggested earlier, getting the ring from True Love Waits means you are stating you believe that in order to have a very fulfilled and fun marriage, you will wait for the one who you marry. When you get engaged, you will replace the True Love Waits ring with your engagement ring. God will reward you more than you will ever know, so please wait on God.

Tip #2: Don't make every thought known, or you might be made out to look like a fool. I do not believe in having a secretive life, and actually I have no secrets about my life. But, I do believe in thinking before you speak! I can give several examples where many times I spoke before I should have. This makes everything complicated, because now you have told another person who will probably tell another, and so on. I would advise you to have two older women who you can tell anything to - your mom, grandma, other woman mentor, or father. These people will know you best, and when you change your mind a thousand times, they are not surprised.

Tip #3: Your parents know you best and are your #1 fan. I have taken my parents on a whirlwind these past two years. I graduated college early and moved to Orlando for what was expected to be only half a year. In July, I decided to stay until December. In December, I decided I might just stay there for another year. So, in the course of a year-and-a-half, I moved to five different places. Then in February, I called my parents and said, "I'm moving to Atlanta in April." My parents know me, and they realize I am a jumping jellybean. They were happy I decided to move back closer to home and just laughed off my crazy journey thus far. When my parents moved me into my fifth place since graduating college, my dad jokingly said, "Ok, we will be back in a month to move you again." I said, "Ha ha, Dad. I hope I am here a little longer this time." The funny and ironic thing was, as I was writing this book, I had to move to a new apartment in Atlanta, because my landlord could no longer rent it. The following week, I was offered a teaching position in Orlando. So, I felt God calling me back to Orlando where I now live. God has a plan and I am just following him (even if I have to move for the 7th time). I guess my dad won that bet.

Tip #4: Always believe you are loved, because YOU ARE! Everyone desires to be loved. Love is so complex. Americans give love only one name, but the Greeks have three different names for love. They are ***Eros, Philea***, and ***Agape. Philea*** would be used to describe the bonds that you have with your friends and the memories you have together. The city of brotherly love, Philadelphia, came from Philea. Philea cannot be reliable, though, because it is based on satisfying a friendship, and sometimes friendships fail or come and go.

Eros stimulates the senses and gives you those butterflies in your stomach. The Roman name for Cupid is Eros. Cupid is the son of Aphrodite, the goddess of love and beauty, and the daughter of Zeus. Eros is when you think someone is super cute, you are infatuated (obsessed, lovesick, crazed over a guy), or when you love to shop or eat chocolate. Eros is only good if the situation is good, but if something goes wrong, Eros love will quickly disappear. Eros is only on the surface and cannot build lasting relationships. It is love from the outward appearance. These are all things you love based on the outside appearance and or taste. I always tell people "I love you" or "I loved what happened today." In other words, I find favor in you right now and you mean a lot to my life. However, things happen and "Eros" love can come and go. Do not let any guy lie to you and tell you that you need Eros, "physical love," to be in a real relationship. In fact, that is so wrong, and he knows it. He is just selfish and wants you to please his desires, on the physical level.

Agape is the last form, and this form of love is unconditional. Agape love can only come from God and the love that is selfless. Agape love is when you forgive others and "love your neighbor as yourself." This is realizing that God sent His only son, Jesus, to die for our sins. God loved (Agape) us by sending His Son. "For God loved the world so much that he gave his one and only Son, so that everyone who believes in him will not perish but have eternal life," John 3:16. Agape love is the only genuine and real type of love, which is hard to have because, as mere mortals, we are selfish. You discover Agape love when someone forgives you for something stupid you have done. You also can show Agape love when someone says something bad about you and you just pray for them and forgive them immediately. Agape love is putting what someone else wants before what you want.

Have you ever experienced Agape love? (Write about it here)

Tip #5: Communication in a relationship is KEY! If you cannot communicate, please BEWARE! A lack of communication equals upset feelings, drama, and heartbreak later on. If you cannot communicate, then there is no way you could marry that person. I promise that if you do not understand one another and everything always gets mixed up when you say something, then if you marry, you will be divorced very soon. It is really important that you figure this out fast. The longer you date, the more your heart gets attached to that person. This is something I had to learn the hard way. I really liked a guy. I liked him a lot! However, any time I would try to tell him how I felt, we would always get in an argument or he said I hurt his feelings. We just did not communicate on the same level, which means that God made someone better for him (who could communicate better and understand him better) and God made someone better for me. I kept thinking we could "work on it." After all, I was a communication major in college. But I learned fast that you cannot change people. They have to change themselves, and you should not want to change the people you are with. You should be proud of them for the way that they are.

Women automatically expect too much from guys. Let's be easy on them and communicate with them if there is something that really bothers us. Women like to talk out their feelings, while guys usually keep what they feel inside. When girls get mad, they tell others, but when guys are upset, they usually retreat to their cave or a quiet place where they can think or get away.

One time, I dated a guy for a year and he never gave me flowers. Finally, on Valentine's Day I asked him why he never gave me flowers. He said that when we first started dating, I had said that flowers were a waste of money. I love flowers and cannot even imagine those words coming out of my mouth. Since we had not communicated well and he did not want to displease me, I had not gotten flowers the entire year. As soon as I told him I actually loved flowers, I received three different flower arrangements in a matter of a month. It is crazy what clear communication can do!

Another tip on communicating is to never criticize your boyfriend in public. Why would you embarrass someone you love and who is one of your best friends? Instead, say good things about him to your friends and brag on him if he just did something awesome. Maybe he helped you study, maybe he hit a homerun at yesterday's game, maybe he sent you flowers or a sweet note. You can brag about anything that meant something to you. If you cannot lift him up in conversations, then he shouldn't be your boyfriend. Also, go ahead and assume he can do everything. Men love it when you think they are Superman! If you need help with something, say, "I know you are great at _____, so can you help me with _____?" Men would rather say, "I can't do that," than have you doubtingly say, "Do you know how to _____?" Men are insecure and need respect, so have confidence in them. If they cannot help you, then say, "No problem, I just thought I would ask you first."

This is a picture of me getting ready to go to a middle school social dance with a guy who asked me out in 5th grade.

Chapter 8

8. Heartbreak

Listen to your heart: Soul Talk

I love this song by Roxette, titled, "Listen to your Heart." The lyrics describe being infatuated (obsessed) by one another's looks; however, the "love falls apart," and in the song it says, "your little piece of heaven turns too dark." Remember, the Bible says, "the heart is the most deceitful of all things," so make sure to only listen to your heart when God is calling for you. This means listening to God's heart, the voices of the Holy Spirit, "that want to be heard," and reading God's word/teachings (the Bible). Following your heart means obeying your feelings instead of God. It is easy to love others when you love God first and you are being obedient to Him.

The heart is so sensitive and fragile. Especially when you are going through your teenage years. I remember wanting and desiring to like a guy, just so my heart would skip a beat if I saw or thought about him. The only problem with this is that you are giving yourself false hope.

You see, culture tells you to pursue a guy, so the quiet way of doing that is by secretly liking them. I promise that if you wait to be pursued and seek God, then God will bring someone very special into our life.

If a guy pursues you and you like him, please do not play hard to get! The world teaches us that when we date we should play mind games - like hard to get - but this is not true at all. Playing hard to get is being disrespectful to the guy that is trying to pursue you. There is a proper balance where you can show interest, but set boundaries so that temptations are minimized. Also, do not get desperate if a guy does not pursue you. Instead, become friends and if he pursues then it will happen, but if he doesn't, then just be friends. If you both are crazy about each other, then be careful by minimizing the temptation. How? You can show him love by serving him in small ways that are not intimate. Stay in public and do not let anything about your relationship be a secret. Secrets get you into trouble. After all, a friendship is what will get you through a marriage, not good looks! Can you respect him? Is he smart? Is he wise? Does he love your character and personality? Is he respectful on your thoughts about sex? Do you communicate well with one another? If you answered yes to all of these questions, then you have a great start to a dating relationship.

The key is to not let your relationship get too physical. I will go more in-depth with this in the sex chapter, but I promise, this one principle will save you from a life of heartbreak. When things get too physical, this is when your heart gets torn, ripped and broken in many pieces. It is like taking a beautiful, perfect piece of white paper and tearing it to shreds. Read what the Bible says about taking part in sexual acts outside of marriage.

"You say, 'I am allowed to do anything' —but not everything is good for you. And even though 'I am allowed to do anything,' I must not become a slave to anything. You say, 'Food was made for the stomach, and the stomach for food." (This is true, though someday God will do away with both of them.) But you can't say that our bodies were made for sexual immorality. They were made for the Lord, and the Lord cares about our bodies," 1 Corinthians 6:12-14.

"Run from sexual sin! No other sin so clearly affects the body as this one does. For sexual immorality is a sin against your own body,"1 Corinthians 6:18.

"But because there is so much sexual immorality, each man should have his own wife, and each woman should have her own husband," 1 Corinthians 7:2.

"And we must not engage in sexual immorality as some of them did, causing 23,000 of them to die in one day,"1 Corinthians 10:8.

If you haven't experienced sexual immorality, then you are very blessed and probably have great parents, mentors or friends watching over you. I want to help keep your beautiful white paper all together in one piece. If you do have a bunch of scraps of white paper lying at your feet, then I will help you pick them up. Let's do the repair work together.

The beauty of the heart is that there is only one way that it can be properly put back together. Would you like to know how? Well, it is actually very simple, but a very bold move you will have to take. Are you ready? It requires that you allow God to enter your heart.

I am not going to pressure you to make a decision now, but just follow me through this thought. You are the only person who can change your mind and make your decisions. People can recommend things, but no one can make you decide. Basically, you have this awesome power of choice and free will. I wish you could talk to the thousands of girls I have talked with over the years, who will tell you that one bad choice can lead to a life full of consequences and despair. Despair is defined in the dictionary as: a profound feeling that there is no hope or that somebody or something makes somebody feel hopeless or exasperated (Encarta®).

So how can you avoid despair? The only answer is to walk with God. Hold His hand and let Him carry you through your days. I always love the illustration of a girl walking down the beach and there is a set of footprints walking beside her, but no person. All of a sudden, there is only one set of footprints, and it is because Jesus picked the girl up and is carrying her down the beach and throughout her life.

Another great example is this very real and true story of Lot's wife, which is found in Genesis 19:15-17 and 26. This lesson is on listening to God and what can happen if you do not. "At dawn the next morning the angels became insistent. 'Hurry,' they said to Lot. 'Take your wife and your two daughters who are here. Get out right now, or you will be swept away in the destruction of the city!' When Lot still hesitated, the angels seized his hand and the hands of his wife and two daughter and rushed them to safety outside the city, for the LORD was merciful. When they were safely out of the city, one of the angels ordered, 'Run for your lives! And don't look back or stop anywhere in the valley! Escape to the mountains, or you will be swept away! (skip to verse 26) But Lot's wife looked back as she was following behind him, and she turned into a pillar of salt."

Luke 17:32-33 also says, "Remember what happened to Lot's wife! If you cling to your life, you will lose it, and if you let your life go, you will save it."

The lesson here is that as daughters of God, which I pray that you believe you are, we must let God guide our path. We never know where the paths we choose will lead, but I can promise you, as the Bible states, if you follow God's path, your life will be priceless. You see, "Wherever your treasure is, there the desires of your heart will also be," Matthew 6:21.

So, if you want all your "daily gift boxes" to be open, then your heart has to be set on God. The only way this can happen is if you believe that God sent His son, Jesus, to be born from Mary, a virgin. Also, that Jesus lived life on earth to be an example to us, and died for our sins, and after three days was raised from the dead.

Jesus experienced the worst and ultimate payment for our sins. He also left the greatest gift behind, which is His Holy Spirit. You see, the moment you believe, the Holy Spirit and Jesus live inside of you forever. Now you are a living, breathing, walking temple of God! "Don't you realize that your body is the temple of the Holy Spirit, who lives in you and was given to you by God? You do not belong to yourself, for God bought you with a high price. So you must honor God with your body." 1 Corinthians 6:19-20.

How incredible! How amazing! How lucky we are! We are so treasured and loved by God! Can you believe God loves you more than anyone else ever could? Can you believe that He made you to represent Him on this earth? Can you believe He will never ever leave you nor forsake you? In other words, God will never ditch you, turn His back on you, abandon you, desert you, or give up on you. How COOL! How AWESOME! How CRAZY FUN is that? "For the Lord is the Spirit, and wherever the Spirit of the Lord is, there is freedom," 2 Corinthians 3:17. You can only trust your heart when you are listening to God and obeying Him. You listen to Him by praying and reading His word (Bible). When you are not obeying God's truth, "the human heart is the most deceitful of all things," Jeremiah 17:9.

Can you believe that your beautiful red heart can be deceitful? "Deceitful" is intentionally misleading or fraudulent in lying to people or not telling them the whole truth (Encarta®). Can you believe that all those fun Valentine's Day traditions, beautiful decorations, and love can all be fake if they are not given from a heart of genuine care for you? The reason they can be fake is because people are expected to give gifts on Valentine's Day. A guy should give you gifts throughout the year and not just on holidays. Gifts can be cooking a meal, bringing you cookies, taking you to get Starbucks, going for a walk, or writing you a letter. I still think you deserve to feel loved on Valentine's Day, but you should also feel loved 364 other days out of the year. Here's a heads up: most guys hate Valentine's Day and have no idea how much girls care about it. It is good to tell them in advance that you would like Valentine's Day to be special and full of surprises, so they know!

Satan not only confuses us with love, but believe it or not, you are being lied to countless times a day. "The heart is deceitful above all things," as we said before. Satan is attacking you and you do not even realize it. He is throwing peer pressure, acceptance, failure, unhappiness, guys, drugs, alcohol, sex, and so much more in your face. Your parents try to protect you by not letting you watch certain TV shows or not letting you go to "R" rated movies, but it still gets to your ears and eyes somehow. Think about how much you watch TV, or how often you look at edited pictures in magazines, or how many girls have had surgery to try to look better, and so much more! In fact, A 1995 study found that three minutes spent looking at models in a fashion magazine caused 70% of women to feel depressed, guilty, and ashamed. Did you know the average American woman is 5'4" tall and weighs 140 pounds? God did not make us clone Barbie dolls and thank goodness, because Barbie, at 5'9" tall and 110 pounds, would have a Body Mass Index of 16.24 and be severely underweight. So much so, that her measurements would be a 39" bust, 18" waist, 33" thighs and a size 3 shoe! If she was real, she would have to walk on all fours, because she wouldn't be able to hold herself up. The sad thing is that every girl would love to look like Barbie and Barbie dolls are sold to girls ages 3 to 12, making a girl at the age of 3 think that Barbie is what is most beautiful. This is so sad to me, because in your teenage years, your body has to grow properly and healthy. If you deprive or rob your body of the essential nutrients when you are growing up, you will have major health problems later in life. Healthy is the way to be and that includes following the food pyramid, eating fruits and vegetables, exercising or playing sports, and staying away from too many non-nutritious snacks and cookies. Those snacks and cookies have lots of sugar that turns into fat. Once you have fat cells, they will never go away, but they can decrease in size. I always reward myself with 2 snacks a day and a sweet treat along with exercise. This way you can fulfill a craving and still be healthy.

Well, I want to feed you the truth about many lies that are attacking you daily. I pray that you will listen to me and that we will be great friends after you have read this book. The truth is that the only perfect love comes from Jesus, who lives in you if you believe. "You are made wonderfully," Psalms 139:14. God made you as His beautiful princess and sent His son Jesus to die and save you. Jesus loves you more than you can ever imagine. Without Jesus' love, love is flawed. Without Jesus, love hurts. Without Jesus, the heart breaks into small crystal pieces that are very hard to put back together. I have to believe that Cinderella, Sleeping Beauty and Snow White all had the perfect love I am speaking of, but they were living in a fairytale. This type of perfect love can only be found between you, God, Jesus and the Holy Spirit. It cannot be found in this world, because we are all sinners and we mess up. So, back to Cinderella, do you know what the definition of a fairy tale is? A fairy tale is a story for children about fairies or other imaginary beings and events, often containing a moral message; or an ***improbable invented account of something***, often a ***false excuse*** (Encarta®).

Let's get personal. The world and your friends believe things that are not true. We believe in fairytales, but the only fairytale you can look forward to is eternity in heaven with Jesus if you believe. The world, TV, magazines, books, movies, and the list goes on, make us believe that life can be perfect or that love is perfect. I believed that, too. But, when you think about being married one day, do you think about arguments that you will get into? Do you think about crying? I cannot think of many celebrities who are still happily married. Can you? The reason is because love is a choice and a decision you make. Yes, there is attraction and a desire to want to know someone more, but every person will disappoint you some time in your life, because no one is perfect. The key is forgiveness, grace, and acceptance. Please do not cheat on your boyfriend if you are unhappy with him. Cheating is a habit that can be addictive, and if you start young, then you have a good possibility of carrying it into a marriage. My cousin taught me a saying "cheaters never prosper." I grew up learning, "Once a cheater, always a cheater." The sad thing is, as I have grown up, I can honestly say both of those sayings are very true. Do not be weak and secretive. If you do not want to date him anymore, then break up with him. But please do not cheat on him. Word will get around fast and he will tell others. All of a sudden, other guys will not trust you and they will think, "What will keep her from cheating on me, too?"

I cannot stand to get into arguments. I really dislike conflict, because I like to be the peacemaker. I will never forget when I dated a guy a year ago and I got very upset. We had driven to the beach and I was planning on breaking up, because we were always disagreeing on things. I was quiet the entire car ride and it just seemed so awkward.

P.S. This is not a recommendation.

So when we got to the beach, I jumped out of the car and ran to the beach. I put my towel on the sand and laid down, trying to forget about how awful this date was with someone I had been dating for three months. He then came up next to me and put his chair down beside me. I turned my head the other way and he said, "Whitney, what is wrong with you? Why are you so upset with me?"

I immediately broke into tears. I mean a waterfall was flowing from my eyes. I was crying because I really cared for him, and I was so upset that we kept disagreeing. I never get into arguments, so it really made me upset when I would get in an argument with someone I was starting to share a small piece of my heart with. (A side note: Only give a guy a small piece of your heart until you marry him. Then he can have the rest of your heart after you give it to God first!) As soon as he saw my tears flowing down my face, he immediately was sitting in the sand next to me, rubbing my back. Wow, this meant the world to me. The person who was making me mad just had the guts to get down and dirty in the sand and was doing all he could to comfort me. At that moment, we both forgot why we were even mad, and apologized.

The point of my story is that my boyfriend would disappoint me and I would disappoint him, but the key is to forgive and forget quickly! If someone is your friend, then he should never want to see you cry, but should desire to always see you smiling!

We can't listen to our world, which makes us think that other people are living perfect, fairytale lives. I know I might sound like your mom, but please stay with me. I am telling you this because I was just in your shoes. I know. I promise. I am now 23 years old and the high school I went to is very much like the movie *Mean Girls*. I felt captive in high school, and it was always hard to be who I wanted to be. I was known as the quiet, shy girl, and I hated that. I wanted to be known as the sweet, fun, pretty girl. Then I went to college, joined a great sorority, and got involved with Christian groups on campus. After graduating college, I participated in the Disney College Program and was trained as a stilt walker for the Walt Disney parades. My mom would always tell me to just get through middle and high school, because she knew that I would do great in the real world. She would encourage me to love God, and I had an amazing group of great Christian friends. All this is to say: I have heard the awful stories of heartbreak. These stories did not start at age 18; they started at age 12. I want to help you avoid this heartache. You would not believe how many messed-up girls are out there. If you are one of those messed-up girls, it is okay, because today is a new day and the beginning of a new life. Pray for a new heart and God will give it to you if you are seeking Him. If you have not messed up, then you are in the amazing 20% of girls that are still pure, virgin Mary's who love God with all their heart, soul, mind, and strength. I bet you grew up in a loving environment and were probably raised in a great church. Many of you might be like me and accepted Christ at the age of 7. The moral of the story is "you can't judge a book by its cover." From the outside, many popular girls look like gorgeous white roses, but on the inside 80% of girls, who have lost their virginity, are struggling and hoping that their roses are not wilting with petals falling off. If you do feel this way, then please talk to a trusted adult figure. You are not meant to struggle through life alone and many people would be excited to help you. If you have earned an A+ in this area, then congratulations and make sure you keep that crown of purity on your head. Do not let ANY guy take that crown off until you get married.

Isaiah 61:1 says, "He has sent me to comfort the brokenhearted." We have to surrender every part of our hurt to Him. Do you know where suicide, drug abuse, divorces, alcoholism, and other awful things often originate? The answer is a broken heart.

The John Mayer song, "Dreaming With A Broken Heart," is about being left with a broken heart. All of a sudden it hits you that your relationship is no longer a dream, but a reality you have to deal with.

This is when Eros love has come to an end, and only God can truly help you recover with his unfailing Agape love. One of the verses is about how "the waking up (giving up) is the hardest part." It is hard when you have given so much of yourself to another and then you feel abandoned when they leave. John Mayer sings about what heartbreak feels like including: being on your knees, feeling like you can't breathe, "crying eyes," and having to say goodbye forever, because he is gone. The good news is that God is *never* gone!

When the Holy Spirit lives in you, He gets down on His knees and comforts you. He helps you put all the pieces of white paper, rose petals, and broken crystal back together. God tells us that He forgives you for EVERYTHING. He loves you more than you will ever know. And you will never wake up to find God gone, gone, gone, gone, gone. He will always say, "Come here, let me hold you, let me love you, and let me wipe away your tears."

He says, "For I know the plans I have for you," declares the LORD. "They are plans for good and not for disaster, to give you hope and a future. In those days when you pray, I will listen. If you look for me wholeheartedly, you will find me," Jeremiah 29:11-13. God will give you a new heart and exchange the old taped-up white paper with a new, clean, and shiny piece of white paper. Let's start over together and learn from other people's mistakes. Together we will say, "Jesus Take the Wheel."

I love this song, because it is about a girl admitting she cannot do it on her own, because she has lost control of her car (which symbolizes her life). We never have control of our life fully. This is a lie we talked about before that the world wants us to believe. We can make choices as we go along, but God always has the keys to our lives. The question is whether you will let Him always keep the keys and drive, or whether you will want to take over and drive. I would recommend always letting God drive!

This describes my life on a daily basis, because I pray and allow God to take the wheel of my life, and then by the end of the day I become the driver again without realizing it. In the song, the girl was scared, so "she threw her hands up in the air" and asked "Jesus take the wheel" and drive her life. She speaks of surrendering to God and begging for a second chance. It is such a sweet reminder to pray when you get in the car and ask God to save you from traps or the "road I'm on." He will gladly sit in the driver's seat and help clean up the mess. Jesus has saved us once and for all, so ask Him to help, because He truly is your Life Savior! It is never too late for Jesus to "take the wheel." I suggest asking Jesus to "take the wheel" every single morning when you wake up and as you walk throughout your day! Your day will start out so much better than you could have imagined. When I would switch classes and walk down the hall at school, sometimes I would pray and feel like Jesus was holding my hand and helping me through the day. Those were my favorite days.

Let your conscience (Holy Spirit) be your guide. "Then you will know the truth, and the truth will set you free," John 8:32. The Bible says, "No eye has seen, no ear has heard, no mind has imagined what God has prepared for those who love him," 1 Corinthians 2:9.

This is a picture of me in one of my ballet dance costumes.

9. I Want It and I Want It Now

If God doesn't give you what you want, do you think God doesn't love you? If God does not let you make the cheerleading team, there is a reason. I did not make the cheerleading team, but instead of getting mad at God, I said, "Thank You, because I know You have something better for me." Do you think God wants what is best for you or what is worst for you? If God made you, then shouldn't God know what is best for you? As the saying goes, "Everything happens for a reason." The important thing is to never get discouraged and try to learn a lesson from your experiences. If you are a fan of the show *Scrubs*, a great example of this is from the episode: *Laverne's Accident.* You can watch it at: *http://www.youtube.com/watch?v=-mAtjs-JAtE.*

We have to be patient and wait. I know waiting is hard, but you will gain a lot of knowledge if you are patient and wait. The Bible talks about the importance of being patient all the time. If you want to learn to trust, then you have to learn how to be patient. I had to be patient with being a performer at Disney, with jobs, and with wanting a dog. God has perfect timing, so if we wait for His right timing, you will never look back and regret. This is when you will really see how things happen for a reason.

I will never forget when I was five years old and I thought my parents had decided that I should be an only child. I had a doll that I carried around everywhere with me. I named her Sister, and because I took her everywhere, Sister was in need of a big makeover. Her hair was failing out. Stuffing was coming out of her and I even think her eye was falling out, but I loved her so much! One day, I decided to ask my parents if they would give me a real sister. My parents whispered for a minute and then said okay. A few months later, my mom told me that I was going to have another sibling. I was so excited about having a sister, but my mom told me I might have a brother.

"Brother? I said I wanted a sister!" I would say, or at least think it.

Then about one month before my other sibling was about to arrive, I changed my mind and told my mom that I wanted a puppy instead. My mom tried to explain that it was too late and that I needed to be excited about having another sibling. I said okay and waited patiently. I was in kindergarten and my teacher was even letting my class do a countdown with numbers on the wall until the day my sibling was to arrive. On September 21, 1992, I leaped off the bus and ran inside my house where my grandma was standing. My grandma, I call her TuTu, which is Hawaiian for grandma, smiled and said, "Do you want to go to the hospital? Your brother is here."

I think in that brief moment my head spun around about 15 times and I did not realize it.

"A brother? I did not ask for a brother!"

I was very disappointed. "How could this be so hard for me to get a sister?" I thought. But as soon as we got to the hospital and I was able to hold my new brother, all my sadness turned into happiness. I was now a BIG SISTER!

You see, God knew what was best for me. Now, looking back on my early years, I am so grateful for a little brother. My brother and I are six years apart, so I helped take care of him, we never argued, and I never had to worry about him stealing my clothes. It was great. He is great! God knows best. I just needed FAITH and TRUST that He would give me what I needed the most. This is a great example of expectations. I demanded God give me a sister and he gave me a wonderful brother named Kyle.

I also had to learn a lesson in patience, because now that I had a little brother, I had to wait four more years until I could get a puppy. After waiting all that time, I was able to get Skipper. He is the best dog ever, and he lies by my side at night until I go to sleep and wakes me up in the morning! Skipper shows me Agape love. I know this sounds funny, but besides wanting food and to go outside to go potty, how selfish is any dog? Skipper is not. You can see love just from looking in his eyes. He is so special to our family. He is my other brother.

If you have strong feelings about something, be silent and talk to God about it, first. See what He says about that in the Bible. Then ask your mom, dad or a mentor what they think about it. The last thing you should do is to tell your friends. You need mature wisdom before you seek uncertain counsel. If you are lonely and long for love, then turn to Jesus. If you are bored, ask someone to go serve with you at the soup kitchen or go visit a nursing home. When you serve others, you will be filled with love and joy. Spending time with God is good (Bible study, prayer, journaling to God), because it makes you think about and grow closer to God. True love is following what God tells you to do, and being grateful and obedient as He guides you.

What do you desire? (Answer below or use this as a topic for your journal entry)

Have you asked God for His will? (Answer below)

Has God ever surprised you? (I sure hope so! Please answer below)

Chapter 10

10. Sex

This is your wake-up call. ***Beep Beep. Beep Beep. Beep Beep.*** "This is your conscience in your head telling you to wake up and do not let a guy lie to you. ***Beep Beep. Beep Beep.***

News Alert! This just in: "More than 750,000 teenage girls will become pregnant this year," according to TroubledTeens.com ("Troubled Teens"). Now, 30% of teen girls in the United States become pregnant at least once before the age of 20. It's alarming, but the breaking news just keeps coming. "In 2007, 48% of high school students reported having had sexual intercourse," according to the Center for Disease Control. They report, "nearly 50% of the 19 million new STD infections are diagnosed in people between the ages of 15 to 24." Many STD infections do not go away and stay in your body forever. Here's a heartbreaker! "Ninety percent of teenage girls who have sex and don't use protection will get pregnant," states the Center for Disease Control and Prevention. (Statistics courtesy of the Centers for Disease Control and Prevention, *StayTeen.org* and the Guttmacher Institute.)

A guy does not want to marry a statistic that fits into the facts above. If you are going to be a good girl with a pure heart, then you are NOT going to fit into the crowd. The truth is the majority of guys really want to marry a virgin. If you are a virgin, you are going to stand out, and this is the most amazing thing that can happen to you. After questioning several great Christian guys, many desire for their future wife to save herself for them. In other words, do not have sex before marriage. They also said, confidence is the key. Our life is short and flies by quickly, so why live a life full of regrets for a few minutes of risky and harmful fun? Guys admire a girl who understands who God made her to be and is confident. Guys love to talk to girls who are themselves and who respect who they are. If you are a sweet girl who takes care of herself and treats everyone with respect, then how could anyone not like you? If they do not like you, it is probably because they are jealous and wish they had made better decisions, like you have. Or, if it is a guy, he is probably intimidated and thinks you are too good for him.

TV and music is not a standard or role model we should follow. According to TroubledTeens.com, "42% of the songs on the top 10 CDs in 1999 contained sexual content, 19% included direct descriptions of sexual intercourse. Also, on average, music videos contain 93 sexual situations per hour, including eleven "hard core" scenes depicting behaviors such as intercourse and oral sex" ("Troubled

Teens"). Many girls believe having sex will make the guy love her and commit to her more. However, the truth is, once you have sex with a guy, he is likely to question whether he can trust you. He does not respect you and wonders "what else has this girl done?" It is a trap that many guys set; and once you fall in, you will have regrets and emotional damage. When guys have sex, they are thinking how good it feels to their body, not about how much they love you. I love this quote from Shaunti Feldhahn that is so true, "You see, the guy is using and taking advantage of you, because, 'girls use sex to get love and guys use love to get sex.' "

Men are also encouraged by their guy friends to have sex. They are competing to see who can have sex with the most girls. The problem is, every time you have sex, you pick up new germs/sexually transmitted diseases from that person. Could you imagine marrying someone who could possibly have 15 different diseases and will give them to you? The other thing is that most guys will not tell you if they have a disease. The way you find out is by being in pain after sex and when you are forced to get prescription medicine from the doctor. According to TroubledTeens.com, "Every day, 8,000 teenagers in the United States become infected by a sexually transmitted disease. This year, nearly 3 million teens will become infected. Overall, roughly one-quarter of the nation's sexually active teens have been infected by a sexually trans-mitted disease (STD)" ("Troubled Teen"). All I can say is that there are SO many positives to not having sex before marriage. No STDs, less heartbreak, a better marriage someday, you won't get pregnant, you will be pure, and God will honor your life and decision. I would not risk it and take a chance; I can tell you the benefits of waiting are INCREDIBLE. I cannot wait to tell the guy I marry that I have waited for him and only him!

If you are dating a Christian guy who has changed his life around or wants to be a virgin until marriage, then I am so proud of you. He is probably a great catch, but you are still going to have to help him out. Guys need your help to protect both of you. It is hard for a guy not to want to have sex, no matter who he is. If you are laying down in bed with him or wearing tight clothes, then you are tempting him. If you really love and cherish your relationship, I would encourage you to avoid these pitfalls and canyons.

Enjoy reading 17-year-old Alex 's story:

Ever since the start of sophomore year, I've surrounded myself with three girlfriends, who we will call Gina, Sally, and Mary to protect their names. I guess I must be doing something right since most girls seem to like me (some just as a friend), but I've found out that success is not dictated by simply having a girlfriend, as several have proven to be fool's gold.

Let's rewind back to August 11, 2008, the day I asked Gina to be my girlfriend. It was nothing romantic, just a simple phone call before she started at a school where some other guy might sweep her off her feet. The relationship started off great, and after a month in, I received my first kiss ever. These "first evers" started happening way too quickly, and before I knew it, all I was looking forward to was the next hook-up. We both got lost in this physical realm, but neither of us seemed to want to talk about it. Then all of a sudden, she took it all away from me (my entire virginity), and because of that, I decided to end the relationship. This was not a good ending by any means! When I called her to say that this was the end, I heard a girl shrieking for breath on the other end. She started whispering that she couldn't breathe, and the tears poured out for what seemed to be a lifetime. She pleaded with me that she had changed, and that I would see a new Gina during the next week, the one I fell in love with. Not knowing what to do, I blindly agreed to continue the relationship for another week. After hanging up the phone that night, I had reached one of the lowliest points of my life, crying on my mom's shoulder for 30 minutes because I knew I wanted to get out and it killed me to hear the girl I had cared for the most cry. Later the next morning, I took the easy way out, sending her a text that I'm sure left some questions unanswered but had closed our door for good.

So with Gina out the door in February, I had a great baseball season and got to spend time with my family and my friends, but the feeling of not having a girlfriend, someone to spend time with who would always be there for me, had left a hole in my heart. So, on June 1, 2009, I asked Sally to fill that hole. I had not consulted anyone on my pick before making it, but I did know that my sister hated her. I just brushed this off, as Sally seemed like the perfect, innocent girl, and was very good-looking! It seemed like smooth sailing, for a while at least, and the first week fell nicely into this category. The summer relationship seemed to be a perfect idea with no school and plenty of hang out time. This "hang out time" turned sour, however, as all she wanted to do was hang out with her reckless friends with bad reputations. I started being extremely quiet whenever we were around them, an attribute that she apparently didn't enjoy too much. So, she in turn became very distant, returning only a select few of my texts and calls.

After that first week, I could tell we just weren't going to work out. I went into the relationship looking for a pure and innocent girl, but I was apparently the only one at school who didn't realize she didn't fit the description. So, right after Independence Day, she broke up with me behind a local ice cream shop. This didn't blindside me, however, as she had treated me badly for three-fourths of our relationship, as well as telling me that we really "needed to talk," and that the talking "wouldn't take too long."

With Sally long out of the picture, I started blindly trying to replace her. Two other crushes that just couldn't seem to get past the first date, or even the first text, ended the summer. Heading into my junior year, I was tired of love, and I just wanted to take the simple approach of being friends with everyone. Apparently one of my good friends didn't have this same thing in mind. I had known of Mary ever since she came to my high school during my freshman year, but during tenth grade, we had become much better friends. During the spring, I had actually had a little crush on her too, but when she found another guy, I decided to look elsewhere. Shockingly to me, she had actually liked me at the same time too, but after thinking it was nonreciprocal, she decided to pursue the other guy. I thank God now so much for us not realizing our love, because during a church retreat called the Walk during the summer of 2009, I fully confessed my broken relationship with Gina, and realized the error of my ways. Upon having this knowledge, I truly believe that Mary and my relationship stayed pure and on the narrow path because of it. So on September 18, 2009, I asked Mary to be my girlfriend, and even though we've had bumps along the way, we've always talked through them and grown much *closer because of it. We've been going out for nine months now, and I would have to say it's because of our three-candle system. By keeping the emotional, spiritual, and physical candles all lit at the same strength, we can overcome almost anything.*

Even though I've been through some difficult relationships, I thank God for the experience I've gained through each one, as I now can see warning signs and learn from my previous mistakes so they don't happen during this relationship. I have fallen hard for my pure and innocent Mary, and I can't wait to see what God has in store for us!

Like Alex mentions in his story, you do not need to be "involved" in a relationship. Instead, you need to be purely loved through an amazing friendship. The Bible even says, "It is not good for a man to touch a woman," 1 Corinthians 7:1 (King James Version). In other words, when you get to a point where you can't keep your hands off each other, then you need to get married. So is this what you really want? I must admit that in every relationship, my boyfriend and I always said "I love you" after a few months of dating; however, to be honest I cared for him "Eros," but never truly loved him as someone I would want to end up with forever "Agape."

As we already talked about, Americans really should adopt the Greeks' words for love. Love is overused and is not as special as it should be. I would recommend using the words enjoy (for Philea type of love), like (for Eros type of love) and love (for unconditional Agape love). Just because I tell my friends I love them all the time, it's different from my love toward God. I want my friends to know I care about them, but instead I should probably say, "I really enjoy hanging out with you" or "you are a great friend." When you tell God you love Him, you should love Him far more than anything else. Waiting until you get engaged to tell a guy you love him will help keep a lot of confusion out of the relationship. It will also be extremely special and unforgettable in a great way.

Every time I get in a dating relationship, I always set boundaries to keep me from being tempted. To many young guys, it is a relief when a girl tells him she doesn't want to kiss, because he finds a mystery in her and that is a surprise and delight. This is how you will STAND OUT ABOVE THE REST.

Flirting also needs to be done in a tactful way, because if you just want attention from the guy, but you would not want to date him, then you are manipulating and teasing him by playing mind games. I have heard several guys make this statement, "An attractive girl is a girl who is real and doesn't need to impress with flirting or other games."

Also, be careful because guys can play games, too. They take advantage of when they need comfort. Many guys like to offer emotional comfort because they know that is the connection they need to make in order to win a girl's heart. If the guy is a typical guy, he is thinking, "If I can comfort her and give her attention, I bet I can get something from her later tonight." Intimacy occurs when two people share their lives through experiences together and deep conversations. Emotional ties are harder to break than physical ties. I am not saying a guy cannot give you advice or help you, but many times it is better to go to an older mentor who always has your best interest at heart. Do not be a victim to Satan and his snares. Always be on guard! Be wise and be classy. Be captivating and intriguing. You are a mystery meant for one and only one very special man.

A very special mentor of mine once said, "Guys, please understand the investment fathers have made in their daughters and show respect for that investment. Don't date to see what you can get out of them." If you did not have an amazing father, then replace this quote with God. God made an incredible investment in you and if a guy does not respect you, then he is making God very angry. I would never want God to be angry with me. Would you?

Another great boundary to set is to not lay next to them. It is okay to hug him, let him put his arm around you, hold hands, cuddle appropriately while watching a movie, but going further will only bring 100% more emotions and heartbreak into your relationship, should you break up. If you value minor physical interaction, then the slightest kisses and sweet hugs will feel like heaven, versus something that is expected. How do you know you want to marry someone just because you have kissed him? You will not know, and your first kiss is always awkward. It is so much better to wait, because intimacy is not necessary! You are wise if you learn to be best friends first and let the smallest touches come later down the road. Kissing and holding hands adds nothing to a conversation (anyone can kiss and hold hands), plus a man of strength would not require that of you.

P.S. Most people date 3-4 people before they end up marrying someone, so do not commit. Like Beyonce says, "If you like it, then you should have put a ring on it."

What if you discover that he is not the one for you? How do you say no? I always ask for God's help, strength, and comfort to guide me. God will always carry you through and help rescue you in uncertain situations.

What are your boundaries? (Please list below 3 areas in your life where you need to set up boundaries)

What do you think about the three-candle system of keeping the emotional, spiritual, and physical candles all lit at the same strength? (Answer below.)

P.S. If you need more space or want to fully commit, I would encourage you to write in a daily journal and write out a promise to God. Write a promise to keep your boundaries and not to go past them. God will honor you and bless you for doing that!

Chapter 11

11. What Else Do Guys Want?

First let me begin by saying that guys are tender and insecure too. Their biggest fear is failure. If they think they will fail in a relationship or they see another better-looking guy competing for a girl, then they will give up. Shaunti says, "Guys look indestructible, but on the inside their hearts are tender, easily hurt, and strongly guarded. However, they will let down their defenses when they know their heart will be safe with a girl." (Feldhahn, *For Young Women Only*) Guys value a girl who is secure in herself and will take care of their heart. They want a girl who is trusting, giving, and genuine. In fact, many guys say that a girl with too much make-up is a turnoff, because she doesn't look real and is not showing her true beauty. A lot of makeup is also a sign of insecurity. Guys also like modesty, because to them if you are modest, then you are an attractive mystery. Modesty is defined as unwillingness to draw attention to your own achievements, looks, and abilities. You can still be a strong woman, with noble character, successful and humble at the same time. These qualities are incredible and admired greatly by men of noble character. If a guy you like is not interested, do not lose heart. Guys cannot force physical attraction, but if you are attractive to them and you have the qualities they are looking for, then be careful, because they may have other thoughts and intentions.

Teenage guys have the biggest egos. The things that my ex-boyfriend in middle school said to me are things an older guy would know better than to say. Plus, a middle school guy would not care about what I would say about him as much as an older guy would. Guys get more insecure when they are older, because they realize they are no longer invincible. Younger guys tend not to admit when they have no clue how to do something. They usually fake it or cover it up by playing the "calm, cool, and collected" card, when in reality, they are clueless. However, older, more humble guys would admit that they do not know how to do what you are asking of them. Older and more mature guys are fearful of what girls might say about them. They have a yearning to perform for a girl they like, and they want to make her laugh.

In fact, everything a guy does, he questions what a girl will think about it and if a girl will respect him for that. They buy material objects to impress a girl (car, speakers, guitar, etc.). They strive to have good judgments and skills/abilities to impress a girl (i.e., athletic, book smart, cooking, musically inclined, etc.).

Guys look for qualities in a girl like having "a passionate love for God" and "a girl who is on my same spiritual level." They also like dating girls who like to do the same activities or hobbies together. It is more fun to do many of those things with another person, especially a girlfriend, rather than by themselves. I love that guys look for this, because it means that they want to spend quality time with you. These qualities are what great Christian guys long for in a girl.

Most men want women to look presentable and feel energetic. God made them in such a way that they really appreciate having beautiful people to look at. Guys also want to be thought of as romantic. They want to be respected, desire to be cared for, and want others to be proud of them. They also want to be proud of you and they should value your character over your appearance. You do not have to be Barbie, but it is important to take care of your body and have a friendly spirit.

Feeling energetic sometimes can be hard if you had a rough day. In my last relationship, the guy always knew when something was wrong. He would say, "You are not yourself today. What's wrong?"

Like every girl, I made the mistake of saying, "nothing." But there was something, even if I did not admit it to myself. I would always get defensive when he would ask, because I wanted to be upbeat and I was sad that he could tell I was not. It was like telling me, "You look bad." In reality, he just wanted to know if there was anything he could do to make me happy and feel better. This was another example of us not communicating clearly.

Cory Montieth, who plays Finn in *Glee*, tells *Seventeen* that the first thing he notices about a girl is, "How she treats other people. And whether she seems happy. I'm always intrigued and interested by people who seem at peace with themselves." When asked what move he would make on a girl, Cory responds, "I just try to make her laugh. That's the best way to make anyone feel comfortable!" (*Seventeen* 126)

Men are also romantic, but many times they are afraid to plan something, because they are afraid we will not like it or will not be impressed. If a girl in their past has been displeased by something great they have tried to do, then they will always be nervous about doing great things for you, too. It is not your fault, but you will have to help build their confidence back up. You should always tell them how sweet it was for them to do what they did, and encourage and appreciate them. Always say thank you, and even send them a text or email letting them know how much it meant to you.

Men take pleasure in looking at good-looking women. To men, you are beautiful and looking at you is like admiring a great art painting. They should respect you and never say anything inappropriate or touch you. You see, when a boy sees a girl he likes, "He can make a choice to dwell on the images and thoughts, or to dismiss them." (*For Women Only,* 123) Between the ages of 11-14, I am sure most guys are still trying to figure this one out, so it is better just to keep your distance and be their friend. The choice they make about whether to dwell on a girl is the critical distinction between temptation and sin. Once an image invades a man's head, he can either dwell on it and possibly even start a mental party, or tear it down immediately and "take every thought captive," as the Bible puts it.

Most men cannot stop involuntary images from popping up in their heads, but men can stop themselves from wanting to look by exercising the discipline to stop looking and thinking about it. On a survey Shanti did, most men who made the choice not to look, regularly attended religious services. And half said they would try to stop themselves from looking. So girls, meeting a guy at church gives you a better chance of being happily married one day.

It is vital that we understand just how much strength and discipline that choice requires, so we can appreciate what our men try to do for us every day in this minefield of a culture (*For Women Only* 123-24). Shanti does say that every man is different in this and she compares it to a dessert party, where one man can't resist the chocolate chip cookies and another man can walk right past them (*For Women Only* 125). A man cannot prevent those initial thoughts or images from intruding.

Don't believe me? Let me illustrate.

Don't read this.

No really, don't read it. Just look at the letters.

Impossible isn't it?

There is no way to notice the letters without reading the word. That's what it's like for a guy. His brain reads "good body" without his even realizing it. (*For Women Only* 120) For us, temptations are not sins. What we do with those temptations is the issue. The Bible states that "Jesus was tempted in every way, and yet without sin," Hebrews 4:15. It is just better to avoid temptations, and the best way is to set up those boundaries we have already discussed.

Lastly, as I have emphasized before, men need respect and affirmation (support). Most men would rather feel lonely and unloved, than to feel inadequate and disrespected. If you want a guy to get angry and start running away, then make him feel like he is insufficient, not good enough, insulted, and nag and complain about him. Women cry when they feel unloved and men get angry when they feel disrespected. Even saying things like, "He's boring," or "He cannot do anything I ask," will make a guy very upset. Be careful, because most guys do not like to show when they are feeling angry or hurt. Guys tend to go to their caves and think about it. But, if you continue to make them feel unvalued, then they will soon give up and break up with you. Instead, you should say, "I am so proud of you" or "I trust you very much." Thank him when he does something for you and ask what he would like to do on your next date night.

12. Purity

This is Craig's story (17 years old):

Whether or not to stay pure is a major decision you will have to make during your teenage years. It is a decision I wish I had made before it was too late. I never went all the way, but regret for what I did do has, at some times, been intense. Coming from someone who has messed up in this area, I just wanted to say that it is not worth it. If I could go back and change that decision, I definitely would.

My freshman year is when I turned away, and made bad decisions relationally. During my sophomore year, I went on a retreat with my school and got baptized about a week later on September 5, 2008. I was going down a wrong path and knew that I needed to make a change. 1 Corinthians 6:18, "Flee from sexual immorality. All other sins as man commits are outside his body, but he who sins sexually sins against his own body."

I also want to say from a guy's perspective what I think of a girl who remains pure. I want my wife to be able to tell me that she has remained pure. That is one thing that I will not be able to tell my wife, and that is something that I really regret. Make the decision now to stay pure; it will make it much easier to say "NO" when you are faced with temptation. If you make the decision to stay pure, you will not regret it.

Safe Sex is no sex. Abstinence is not participating in sex.

Plan ahead and in advance like Craig suggests!

So what happens if I have sex before I am married?

What happens is a life of regret, worry, and guilt.

Here is Dylan's story:

I am no expert when it comes to relationships. I have had a few relationships that became serious. I would always tell my girlfriend, "I do not drink and I don't have sex." Drinking makes you lose control over life, and I never felt comfortable about that. However, peer pressure got the best of me at a party that I should not have gone to. Life is already very difficult, especially as a teenager, and alcohol just makes things worse. The regrets are from a summer party at my friend's house. I could have been talked into anything and was pressured to drink a little at this party. I sat next to a popular girl who was also drinking and the next minute we were kissing. I knew it was wrong, but I couldn't stop. One thing led to another and we ended up in a bedroom. I was definitely out of my comfort zone, all because the alcohol let my boundaries down. Afterwards, I felt awful. I have always been the big brother to everyone, so I felt very guilty for what I had done. I really let a lot of people down.

People thought differently of me, but I still felt like myself. I simply "messed up" and made a mistake. I asked God for forgiveness and He forgave me, because that's why Jesus died on the cross. All I could do was say, "Thank You for forgiving me." My virginity is very important to me, because it is something you can't get back once it's lost. I want to save myself for my wife. I've always pictured myself telling my new bride on our wedding night, lying in bed, saying, "You know what? I have been waiting for you." Being the son of a broken family, I know the hardships of divorce. I believe being a virgin will definitely decrease the chance of divorce. It will make my wife feel so special, knowing I waited for her. Luckily, God gave me this idea at a young age. I remember one of the church leaders, Ben, saying, "God says sex is powerful...but it's meant for marriage."

Sex is made to look so cool, but to be truthful, most guys do not trust you after you have had sex with them. Why, you ask? Because they figure that if you had sex with them before you are married, what would keep you from having sex with another man before you are married? The fact is that all men think about is sex. To be exact, men think about sex on average every eight minutes. Sex is what they want and that is how God made them. Don't ask me why, but that is just how it is. However, God designed girls to be a beautiful mystery to men. A mystery they want to pursue and learn more about. Your job is to help them with their struggle of wanting sex by not tempting them. I realize that many things tempt men, but certain things can really make them stumble. For example, extremely short shorts, showing cleavage/your breasts, talking to them in an alluring (meaning: extremely attractive, tempting, or glamorous, and able to arouse strong desire in people <Encarta®>) way, lying down beside them, and making out with them (kissing them intensely).

Many times, guys will then brag about having sex with you and tell all their friends. The worst part is that this gets all around the school and then your friend tell their mother and eventually your parents find out, whether you already told them or not. The scary thing about pre-marital sex (sex before marriage) is that you have made the biggest commitment to someone you could ever make and he has no obligation to you. Obligation meaning: he has no responsibility or agreement that would force him to continue to love you or stay with you.

I know many times this is very hard to believe, because TV and magazines make it sound like the thing you should do if you want to fit in. You also do not want to be dumped by the guy you like, or you want to be the cool girl in school. However, what is really happening is that you are trying to control your life and grant all YOUR desires. There is no desire for God's plan. Besides, you cannot control other people. My question is: If you really love this person and he can't wait to have sex until he is married, then why do you think he would marry you? If he really loves you, then he will wait! I PROMISE!

Also, did you know that sex protection is not 100% guaranteed? Some men may also have many sexually transmitted diseases that they do not even know they have. I have had friends who had sex for the first time and end up getting a disease for life. Besides pregnancy risks, if I were you, I would not trade 30 minutes of awkward sex — which is what sex is: awkward — for 70 years of being free of sexually transmitted diseases.

Sign a body peace treaty: *www.Seventeen.com/bodypeace*

Chapter 13

13. Peer Pressure (Drugs, Homosexuality, Gossip)

First of all, I want to begin this chapter by listing three phrases that most adults in the business world use to describe teenagers. They are: disrespectful, bad morals, and no work ethic. Ouch! I am included in your generation, and that hurts. The truth is that statistics prove adults' presumptions correct. It is sad, but teenagers spent $5.5 billion on alcohol last year; there are 3,000 new teenage smokers per day; teens watch an average of seven hours of TV per day; teens spend an average of only 38 minutes per week in meaningful conversation with their parents, and send on average 1,800 texts per month. Basically, these statistics prove that teens have bad conversational skills, do not respect adult figures, and spend their time in unlawful activities. This is very sad to me, but the point of this chapter is to tell you that you need to stand out and not be one of these statistics! (Wood, Tough Questions)

I understand that texting is very important, but the point is to make sure that you do not forget how to have a normal conversation with others and not to text while driving. Today, 25% of teen accidents occur because of texting. I realize that we all believe that nothing bad will happen to us, but what if texting caused a driving accident that killed another person? What if driving drunk killed another person?

I am really sorry that we have to talk about drugs, alcohol and making poor decisions, but believe it or not, you will hear about drugs and alcohol in high school, if not in college. The key is to STAY AWAY. You cannot just try them once, because they are addictive. And once you try them, people will expect you to do it again. It is a Grand Canyon that you will fall into, and it is extremely hard to climb up, so why even fall? I am telling you these statistics so that you will stay far, far away from the canyon and tell your friends to run away from it too!

In 2008, almost 33.3% of U.S. teens (age 12 to 17) drank alcohol in the past year, with an average of 4.6 drinks per day, making them drunk and very sick. According to the 2008 National Survey on Drug Use and Health, 8 million adolescents aged 12 to 17 drank alcohol in the past year. Many times abusing alcohol can lead to throwing up, having to have your stomach pumped at the hospital, drunk driving, and bad choices you will always regret. Not to mention that you can easily be arrested and taken to jail. Once a girl drinks, people (including your friends) will talk. They will tell others that you had a drink, and all of a sudden you are known for drinking alcohol. You might think this is cool and will make you popular, until one of these really bad things happens. Then, you will want to join me up on stage, begging girls not to start! I cannot think of one person in my high school who drank alcohol and has not suffered from it. Poor choices early on lead to poor choices later, too. There is no benefit to drinking alcohol. It just makes you lose control of your body.

Around 20% of teens used an illegal drug (there are many, and they all cause major health problems, including making you go crazy in the head). This causes some people to end up in a mental hospital when they are only 20 years old. The Treatment Episode Data Set reported that, in 2008, there were 141,683 admissions of teens to substance abuse treatment programs. (*The OAS Report 2010,* Substance Abuse and Mental Health Services Administration)

According to the Office of Applied Studies (April 29, 2010) Report, 16.6% of teens smoked cigarettes, with an average of 4.4 cigarettes per day. Four million teens smoke cigarettes in a year. The Drug Abuse Warning Network estimates that in 2008 there were about a quarter of a million drug-related emergency department visits by teens. The Drug Abuse Warning Network estimates that, on any given day in 2008, there were 63 emergency department visits for drug-related suicide attempts among teens. (*The OAS Report 2010,* Substance Abuse and Mental Health Services Administration)

In addition, on an average DAY during the past year, the following number of teens ages 12 to 17 have used the indicated substances:

- 1,021,853 smoked cigarettes; 3,845 smoked cigarettes for the first time
- 508,329 drank alcohol; 7,540 drank alcohol for the first time
- 563,182 used marijuana;
- 36,572 used inhalants;
- 24,737 used hallucinogens;
- 16,622 used cocaine;
- 2,866 used heroin; and
- 4,365 used a prohibited drug for the first time.

I love you, so please do not drink alcohol before you are 21. The Bible is full of wisdom and says:

Ephesians 5:17-18 says, "Don't be drunk with wine, because that will ruin your life. Instead, be filled with the Holy Spirit."

1 Thessalonians 5:7-11 says, "Night is the time when people sleep and drinkers get drunk. But let us who live in the light be clearheaded, protected by the armor of faith and love, and wearing as our helmet the confidence of our salvation."

Homosexuality

Neuroscientists believe external emotional (not feeling loved or accepted) and social factors (parents, friends, etc.) greatly influence the developing brain of teenagers. Many teens have rough lives that transform them into rough adults. If they grew up around drugs, alcohol, smoking, abuse, or other horrible things, then they have more emotional issues to overcome than someone who grew up in a stable and loving family. Many times, guys become homosexual because they did not feel the love of their father and, therefore, they look for that love in other men instead of women. This is so sad to me, because a great father would have turned them out to be a completely different person. Homosexuality is just one sin among many. However, God does call it a sin. Homosexuality is not part of God's design for us and it is a sinful practice in His eyes. It is not acceptable to God and is like an addiction. God can heal those who want to confess their sin and change their ways.

Another thing I want to address is the issue of girls kissing and making out with other girls. The worst part is that girls do this in front of other guys to make them excited. Please never stoop that low to impress a guy. If a guy thinks that is cool than he definitely is not the right guy. God made guys to fall in love and marry one girl and God made girls to fall in love and marry one guy. Period! Please do not fall into the traps of this world. They have terrifying consequences. I have a video I would love to show you from a taping of "The Doctor's" TV show. If you come to a workshop, then I will show the video. During the show, they interviewed young teenage girls who are doing stuff just to be cool. It is the saddest thing I have seen in a long time and I hope God will open their eyes to the truth soon. Otherwise, they will probably die of a disease.

God specifically created man for woman and woman for man:

> *Genesis 2:24-25 (NIV) says, "For this reason a man will leave his father and mother and be united to his wife, and they will become one flesh. The man and his wife were both naked, and they felt no shame."*

> *1 Corinthians 6:9-10 says, "Don't you realize that those who do wrong will not inherit the Kingdom of God? Don't fool yourselves. Those who indulge in sexual sin, or who worship idols, or commit adultery, or are male prostitutes, or practice homosexuality, or are thieves, or greedy people, or drunkards, or are abusive, or cheat people —none of these will inherit the Kingdom of God."*

I already discussed in the intro how much peer pressure weighs us down. You should not feel pressured to do anything, but rather act appropriately so that others trust your judgment and confidence and do not pressure you. Girls can be so ugly and rude to one another. This is what guys hate about the way girls act toward one another. They cannot stand that girls judge other girls instead of accepting them. They cannot stand that girls argue instead of love. They cannot stand that girls gossip about one another to make themselves look better. They despise the jealousy and grudges girls have toward other girls.

Guys do not understand why girls are not secure and happy about how beautiful God made them.

Remember: guys think of girls as beautiful paintings, especially if they are beautiful on the inside. Guys cannot stand the outright mean-ness and treatment that girls will give to one another, like in the movie *Mean Girls.* I think the reason girls judge and make assumptions is because they do not have the guts and security to ask, confront, or face each other to figure out what is true and what is not. This causes dis-trust and many hurt feelings. Great, genuine, and loving guys like sweet and loving girls! Just remember, a mean girl makes one mean woman.

Chapter 14

14. Metamorphosis Take 2

In middle school and high school, I was in a group of six amazing girls. Every Friday night we would go to my friend's house and spend the night together. She had the sweetest parents who would cook for us and always make us feel welcome. Plus, her house had a basement, which was where all our girl talk took place. I will never forget about how much we talked about our fear of one day having to go to the gynecologist or woman's doctor. It was a topic that would come up every Friday night. I don't know why, but it did. We all were very innocent, and as each of us would learn things along the way, we would share them. It was like the *Sisterhood of the Traveling Pants*, except we stayed in our hometown.

The bottom line is that life is full of awkward moments. You just have to learn how to embrace them. Sleepovers are also great bonding moments but, of course, I mean girls only!

Also, your skin is about to get very oily, and these red, ugly things called pimples will start forming. Acne is a skin disease that can happen anywhere on the body. It occurs when your pores are clogged with too much oil. This causes your pores to burst and become inflamed — in the form of whiteheads, blackheads or pimples.

You will also begin sweating more often. The key is to stay hydrated and drink lots of water. (About eight cups of water per day.) Sweating, or glistening as I call it, usually happens when your body is getting heated or when you get nervous/anxious. Sweating is great because it cools your body down and keeps you from having heat exhaustion. According to *www.gurl.com*, the average person sweats around four cups a day. I would advise always putting on deodorant in the morning and carrying a mini deodorant in your purse to apply during the day. *Gurl. com* also states, "Deodorant does not block sweat. Instead, it neutralizes odors and fights bacteria." Deodorant is necessary for keeping your body clean and sanitary. (Alloy Media)

Nancy tells girls on *http://www.sexetc.org* of her worries when she was a teenager and the things she went through are the same things every girl faces:

I thought that I was the only girl who grew hair in strange places, found yucky stuff in my underwear and had deep dents on my thighs. And as a teen, I had no way of knowing if the day-to-day worries like bad breath, embarrassing nipple hair, ashy skin or heavy cramps were normal. So, I assumed I was the only one doomed to suffer from them. (Durvasula)

She later says, because "none of my issues were ever publicly discussed, I thought that my original assumption was correct: I was a gross girl with lots of odd problems."

This is why I am writing about these issues in the book. You are normal and are wonderfully made. Please do not get down on yourself, which can lead to low self-esteem and eating disorders that cause major health problems. You are incredible and I hope you realize this!

15. The Parentals

"Children, always obey your parents, for this pleases the Lord. Fathers do not aggravate your children, or they will become discouraged," Col 3:20-21.

Do you remember when you were a little girl and you never wanted to leave your parent's side? If you got lost in the grocery store, it was the scariest thing ever! Our mothers are responsible for teaching us how to grow up and take care of ourselves. They also enjoy taking care of us. We watch everything they do, and many times our mothers show us what God's true love looks like. Do you remember when you got sick and your mom was right there to clean up the mess, or maybe when you were little and your parents changed your diapers? They have had to do some pretty unpleasant things for you, but they do it because they love and care for you.

Little girls also need their fathers to give them attention and take care of them. They need their daddy to tell them that they are beautiful and loved. They need a father who is proud of them, delights in them, and cares for them. Every little girl was made to live in a world with a father who loves her unconditionally. We were meant to know a father's love, be kept safe in it, be protected by it, and blossom there. (*Captivating*,106) A girl needs a daddy who is strong and hard-working. How your father loves you will affect you for good or bad. If your dad gives you a lot of love, attention, assurance, enjoyment, approval, closeness, and care at an early age, you will most likely "suffer less from eating disorders or depression and develop a strong sense of personal identity and positive self-esteem." There is a core part of our hearts that was made for Daddy. Made for his strong and tender love (*Captivating*, 107) Ask your dad to take you to dinner, or go shopping, go fishing, go golfing and let you drive the golf cart, or go for a bike ride together. Spend time with your father and get to know him. If your dad did not have a loving father, then sometimes the girl has to let her father know how much she cares, loves, and wants to hang out with her daddy. No girl should ever be too cool to hang out with her earthly or heavenly father.

There are so many struggling women because there were so many wounded girls (*Captivating*, 64). Girls who are wounded by divorce, abuse, not being told they are beautiful, not being fought for or loved by fathers or others. I never liked to cry and my mom never cried in front of me. I would always cry when I went to sleep if I was upset about something when I was little. In life, girls are told to be secretive and not open. We think that hiding our past will never show, but actually it shows in your actions, reactions, body language, and personality. You are safer by being open and honest, than by pretending you are someone you are not. All guys will agree that one of the most attractive qualities about a girl is a girl who is herself, comfortable and secure in herself.

It is okay to talk to your mom about sex and other girl things. If you go to your mom with sex questions, you will be less tempted to have sex and will have more wisdom. Your mom can even tell you why she waited, or her regrets if she did not. If you ask your friends, they are just as clueless as you are. Even if they have had sex, they may or may not tell you how much their heart is breaking right now. Your mom has obviously had sex, because she had you, and she can tell you that God created it for married adults, not teenagers. I know TV is telling you it is cool, but it is telling you lies.

I just watched a popular teenage show this past summer, and my jaw dropped when I saw that they were challenging each other to have sex. Then, just yesterday, I turned on another show that confirmed society today. It was about teenage girls who were pregnant and were also living with their boyfriends. The show did have a good aspect to it, since it was encouraging the teenage moms to give their babies up for adoption to caring families who couldn't have children. Just remember when you are asked or tempted to have sex say, "I have already won, because I am better than that. I am waiting to give that special gift to only one person and that will be my wedding gift to him." If you already have had sex, you can ask God to give you a new heart and start fresh. Then, when you are tempted, tell yourself the same thing I stated above. Be STRONG, because you are! With God's help, you can do all things, because of His strength. (Philippians 4:13)

Most men would be very impressed by that response to wait and trust you 100 times more. It is said, "eighty percent of girls have sex before age 19" (*Parenting Book*, 12) Please hold out and put yourself in that very special 20% that is waiting. You will never regret it! I am telling you about sex so that your heart will be more pure, because you have an understanding of God's plan for sex only inside a marriage. I cannot tell you how many guys have complimented me for staying pure, and I have never had anyone make fun of me. If anything, guys will like you more because you are rare! You are a sparkling diamond in the rough and a diamond worth fighting for!

Chapter 11

Final Words and Fun Ideas

I want to share my present personal life with you. After I finished writing this book this past summer in a matter of one month, I read over it and said, "I did not write this, God did!" I thought to myself how crazy it was that God just told me what to say and I typed it. You might not believe this, but I promise it is true. In the midst of writing this, I was going through a break-up that required a lot of strength. I can say that God was the one who truly gave me the strength I needed to wait for the right person. God will give you that strength too, if you ask for it. When I finished writing the book, God just spoke to numerous people who wanted to help get the word out. I was so shocked that I did not have to ask many people for any help. God brought them to me. Please look over the acknowledgements to see the people God used to help carry out the final stages of this book. Thank You! Lastly, I want to tell you during the month I was writing this book, I was looking for a full-time job after college and my Disney internship. It was a time of much uncertainty, but every time I began to worry, I asked God for peace, protection, and joy. He always gave it and I am so thankful. Toward the end of July, I was offered a job I really wanted last year. It is a teaching position at a Christian School in Orlando, FL. I was so excited and overwhelmed by God's perfect timing. He sent me to Atlanta to write a book and spend a summer with great people there, and just when I had finished the book and was required to move to a new apartment, God provided my present dream job. WOW! Follow God and I promise He has an incredible plan you cannot even imagine!

To conclude this book, I want to tell you what you can do when you are dating a great guy. There are so many incredible things to do together and I want to give you some ideas. I will give you a Top Ten list of fun dates you can have. Enjoy!

Top Ten Dates

10. Go Bowling with a great group of friends; or go mini golfing and grab ice cream afterwards.
9. Enjoy a bike ride, canoe / kayak ride, white water rafting, hiking, tubing, or any nature activity around where you live.
8. Go on a picnic to a park on a Saturday if it is nice outside. Bring along a Frisbee or football.
7. Enjoy working out together by going for a run, walk, swimming, throwing a football or baseball around, doing gym workout or

drills together. This allows you to encourage one another, stay in shape, and have fun at the same time.

6. Go to a festival, carnival, zoo, museum, or event together that is happening in your town or city. A calendar of events will be in the Sunday's paper.

5. Celebrate holidays together by seeing Fireworks on the Forth of July, Carving a pumpkin together around Halloween, Surprising each other on Valentine's Day with goodies, and making Christmas cookies around Christmas and Decorating Eggs around Easter.

4. Go eat at a fun restaurant where someone is singing or there is a fun environment. Most Mexican restaurants have entertainment or huge crowds on Friday and Saturday nights.

3. Go to a concert or a professional sport's game together.

2. Volunteer together in the community. (ex. Help out at a soup kitchen one Saturday morning)

1. Go to church together and join a Sunday school class if they have one so you can meet other believers. If they just have church, then go to church and grab lunch afterwards.

Things to do for your boyfriend that he will enjoy!

10. Make him cookies, brownies, a cake, or pack him a lunch.

9. Cook dinner for him at your house. Guys LOVE food!

8. Tell him that he looks great today or congratulate him on something he has done well in.

7. Go to his sports games, concerts, or whatever hobby he might be involved with.

6. Ask him to show you how to do something he loves to do.

5. Give him a framed picture of the two of you after a month or 2 months together.

4. Thank him for everything he does to help you and how he makes you feel special.

3. Send him an e-card for any occasion. Decorate his locker for his birthday.

2. Buy him a small gift if you are on a trip or in the mall and you see something that would be perfect for him.

1. Go to dinner at his favorite place or go to his favorite sport's game. (You can even wear a shirt, jersey, or hat with the team's logo on it!)

Good luck girls! I hope this book inspired you to stay pure, be bold, be yourself, and trust in the Lord with all your heart. I would love to hear from you and connect with you at (passionpuritypopularity@gmail.com or www.passionpuritypopularity.com). God is so good to us all if we let him take control and direct our paths. I will be praying for you and I truly hope this book brought more clarity to the lies and traps of this world. I believe in you and know you will impact the world in mighty ways. God Bless!

Resources/End Notes

Alloy Media. (2001). *Share your body image woes or wonders.* Retrieved from *http://www.gurl.com.*

Benson, Elisa. "Have Your Hottest Summer hookup!" *Seventeen* June/ July 2010: 96-98. Print.

Chapman, Gary. *The Five Love Languages.* Chicago: Northfield Publishing, 1992. Print.

Durvasula, Sharanya. "Girls and Body Drama." *Sex, ect.* 09 May 2008: Web. 15 Jun 2010. *http://www.sexetc.org/story/body_image/4678*

Eldredge, John, and Stasi Eldredge. *Captivating: Unveiling the Mystery of a Woman's Soul.* Nashville: Thomas Nelson Publishers, 2005. Print.

Ethridge, Shannon, and Stephen Arterburn. *Preparing Your Daughter for Every Woman's Battle: Creative Conversations About Sexual and Emotional Integrity.* 2nd. Colorado Springs, Colorado: Waterbrook Press, 2010. Print.

Elliot, Elisabeth. *Passion and Purity: Learning to Bring Your Love Life Under Christ's Control.* 2nd. Grand Rapids, MI: Fleming H. Revell, 2002. Print.

Elliot, Ted, Script. *Shrek.* Dir. Andrew Adamson and Vicky Jenson." Perf. Diaz, Cameron, and Mike Myers. DreamWorks Pictures: 2001, Film.

"Exercise to Relieve Stress and Relax the Body." *HowToBeFit.Com.* Team Howtobefit, n.d. Web. 24 Jun 2010. <http://www.how-tobefit.com/exercise-to-relax.htm>.

Feldhahn, Shaunti. *For Young Women Only: What You Need to Know About How Guys Think.* Sisters, Oregon: Multnomah Publisers, Inc., 2006. Print.

Gandhi, Neha. "Seventeen's Hot Guys of Summer." *Seventeen* June/ July 2010: 113-128. Print.

Holy Bible, New Living Translation, copyright 1996, Tyndale House Publishers, Inc.

Kelly, Bill, Script. *Enchanted.* Dir. Kevin Lima." Perf. Adams, Amy. Walt Disney Studios: 2007, Film.

Mayer, John. "Dreaming with a Broken Heart." Continuum. Columbia Records, 2006.

Moore, Beth. *So Long, Insecurity: You've Been a Bad Friend to Us.* Illinois: Tyndale House Publishers, Inc., 2010.

Roxette. "Listen to Your Heart." Look Sharp. EMI, 1988.

Soukhanov, Anne. *Encarta® World English Dictionary.* Bloomsbury Publishing Plc, 1999. Microsoft.

Substance Abuse and Mental Health Services Administration, Office of Applied Studies. (April 29, 2010). *The OAS Report: A Day in the Life of American Adolescents: Substance Use Facts Update.* Rockville, MD.

"Troubled Teens Statistics - Teen Help for Troubled Teens." *Troubled Teens*. TroubledTeens.com, 2010. Web. 23 Jun 2010. <http://www.troubledteens.com/troubled-teens-statistics.html>.

Sampson, Gordie. "Jesus, Take the Wheel." Lyrics. Some Hearts. Arista, 2005.

"Why We Love: The Nature and Chemistry of Romantic Love," by Dr. Helen Fisher. Henry Holt and Company, New York.

Wood, Browning, Perf. *Tough Questions: What About Youth Culture?* First Presbyterian Church of Orlando: 2009, Web. 15 Jun 2010. *http://fpco.org/Seek/Multimedia.aspx?id=441.*

LaVergne, TN USA
15 November 2010
204910LV00004B/94/P